SPECIAL PLAC

ALASTAIR SAWDAY'S
SPECIAL PLACES TO STAY

SPAIN

All the bustling, colourful vitality of
Spain in over 360 stunning places.

EDITED BY JOSE NAVARRO

£14.99

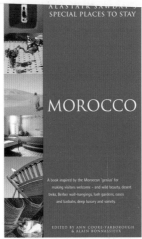

ALASTAIR SAWDAY'S
SPECIAL PLACES TO STAY

MOROCCO

A book inspired by the Moroccan 'genius' for
making visitors welcome – and wild beauty, desert
treks, Berber wall-hangings, lush gardens, oases
and kasbahs, deep luxury and variety.

EDITED BY ANN COOKE-YARBOROUGH
& ALAIN BONNASSIEUX

£10.99

ALASTAIR SAWDAY'S
SPECIAL PLACES TO STAY

INDIA

Irresistible – and a first! An absolutely fascinating
collection of places to stay all over India.

EDITED BY TOBY SAWDAY

£10.99

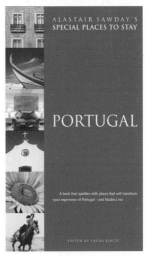

ALASTAIR SAWDAY'S
SPECIAL PLACES TO STAY

PORTUGAL

A book that sparkles with places that will transform
your experience of Portugal – and Madeira too

EDITED BY LAURA KINCH

£10.99

Credit card orders (free p&p for UK orders)
01275 464891
www.specialplacestostay.com

First edition
Copyright © June 2005
Alastair Sawday Publishing Co. Ltd
Published in June 2005
Alastair Sawday Publishing Co. Ltd
The Home Farm Stables,
Barrow Gurney, Bristol BS48 3RW
Tel: +44 (0)1275 464891
Fax: +44 (0)1275 464887
Email: info@specialplacestostay.com
Web: www.specialplacestostay.com

Design:
Caroline King

Maps & Mapping:
Maidenhead Cartographic Services Ltd

Printing:
Butler & Tanner, UK

UK Distribution:
Penguin UK, 80 Strand, London

A catalogue record for this book is
available from the British Library.

Sevan and Müjde Nişanyan have asserted
their rights to be identified as the
authors of this work.

ISBN 1-901970-68-X

Paper and Printing: We have sought the lowest
possible ecological 'footprint' from the
production of this book, using super-efficient
machinery, vegetable inks and high
environmental standards. Our printer is ISO
14001-registered. See inside for details.

The publishers have made every effort to
ensure the accuracy of the information
in this book at the time of going to
press. However, they cannot accept
any responsibility for any loss, injury
or inconvenience resulting from the
use of information contained therein.

ALASTAIR SAWDAY'S
SPECIAL PLACES TO STAY

TURKEY

Contents

Back

Photo Turkish Culture & Tourism Office

Alastair Sawday Publishing

We began by chance, in 1993, seeking a job for a friend. On my desk was a file: a miscellany of handsome old houses in France, some that could provide a bed, and some a meal, to strangers.

I ran a small travel company at the time, taking people off the beaten track; these places were our 'finds'. No chain hotels for us, no tourist restaurants if we could possibly visit old manor houses, farms and châteaux whose owners would breathe new life into our enthusiasm for France.

So Jane set off with a file under her arm and began to turn it into a book. We were then innocent enough to ignore advice and print 'far too many' – 10,000. We sold them all, in six months – and a publishing company was born.

We exhorted readers to enjoy a 'warm welcome, wooden beams, stone walls, good coffee' and nailed our colours firmly to the mast: 'We are not impressed by TVs, mini–bars and trouser-presses'. We urged people to enjoy simplicity and authenticity and railed against the iniquities of corporate travel. Little has changed.

Although there are now more than 25 of us working out here in our rural idyll, publishing about 20 books, we are holding tightly to our original ethos and gradually developing it. Our first priority is to publish the best books in our field and to nourish a reputation for integrity. It is critically important that readers trust our judgement.

Our next priority is to sell them – fortunately they sell themselves, too, such is their reputation for reliability and for providing travellers with memorable experiences and friendships.

However, publishing and selling books is not enough. It raises other questions: what is our impact on the world around us? How do we treat ourselves and other people? Is not a company just people working together with a shared focus? So we have begun to consider our responses to those questions and thus have generated our Ethical Policy.

There is little intrinsically ethical about publishing travel guides, but there are ways in which we can improve. Firstly, we have worked hard to find the paper and printing system with the lowest overall ecological 'footprint'. Secondly, we are promoting local economies and encouraging good work. We seek beauty and are providing an alternative to the corporate culture that has done so much damage. Thirdly, we celebrate the use of

Who are we?

locally sourced and organic food among our owners and have launched a Fine Breakfast scheme in our British bed & breakfast guides.

But the way we function as a company matters too. We treat each other with respect and affection. An easy-going but demanding office atmosphere seems to work for us, as do the four dogs. But for these things to survive we need to engage the staff, so we have created the Green Team and the Charitable Trust team.

 Each team meets monthly to advise the company. The Green team uses our annual Environmental Audit as a text and monitors progress.   The Trust team allocates the small sum that the company gives each year to charities, and raises extra money. On top of all that, the Management Team considers ethical matters and advises the Board.

A few examples of our approach to company life: we compost our waste, recycle the recyclable, run a shared car to work, run a car on LPG and another on a mix of recycled cooking oil and diesel, operate a communal organic food ordering system, use organic or local food for our own events, take part in Bike to Work day, use a 'green' electricity supplier, partially bank with Triodos (the ethical bank in Bristol), have

Photo Paul Groom

a health insurance scheme that encourages alternative therapies, and sequester our carbon emissions.

Especially exciting for us is an imminent move to our own eco offices; they will conserve energy and use little of it. But I have left to the end any mention of our most tangible effort in the ethical field: our Fragile Earth series of books. There are *The Little Food Book*, *The Little Earth Book* and T*he Little Money Book* – hugely respected and selling solidly. Look out for new titles in the Fragile Earth series.

Perhaps the most vital element in our growing Ethical Policy is the sense of engagement that we all have. It is not only stimulating to be trying to do the right thing, but it is an important perspective for us all at work. And that can only help us to continue to produce beautiful books.

Alastair Sawday

Acknowledgments

Sevan Nişanyan wrote to us to ask us to buy the rights to his well-established book, *Küçük Oteller Kitabi*: The Little Hotel Book. We were hesitant, for we like books to be 'ours'. But he persisted, eventually saying, "I am coming over to see you". Still resisting, we said, "Don't! We'll be in touch next week." Well, the following Monday morning, lo and behold – he was here!

He was clearly slightly unusual, and we liked him. But apart from being unusual he also struck us as driven, talented, articulate and cultured, and massively enthusiastic. Most importantly, we agree on the meaning of 'special'; our criteria are identical. So rather than buy his rights we adopted him, and his delightful wife, Müjde, as our 'authors'. We are lucky indeed, for they are fun to work with and bring massive integrity and knowledge to a field, 'accommodation with human contact', in which they have been Turkish pioneers.

Alastair Sawday

Series Editor
Alastair Sawday

Authors
Sevan and Müjde Nişanyan

Editorial Director
Annie Shillito

Production Manager
Julia Richardson

Managing Editor
Jackie King

Web & IT
Russell Wilkinson, Chris Banks, Brian Kimberling

Production
Paul Groom and Allys Williams

Copy Editors
Ann Cooke-Yarborough and Jo Boissevain

Sales & Marketing & PR
Siobhán Flynn, Andreea Petre Goncalves, Sarah Bolton

Accounts
Sheila Clifton, Bridget Bishop, Christine Buxton, Jenny Purdy, Sandra Hasell

A word from Alastair Sawday

Turkey seen through the eyes of Sevan and Müjde Nişanyan is a country of irresistible attractions. But why does Turkey evoke such confused feelings in us? It is hard, it seems, to get a proper feel for the place. Perhaps I am speaking for myself, though the complex question of Turkey's entry to the EU shows how hard it is for us to 'know' her.

I long ago spent a wonderful holiday near Bodrum, in a village of astonishing loveliness and simplicity. I have been to Istanbul and Ankara, and have worked in the far east of Turkey on a disaster relief project with Oxfam. But I have never felt clear about Turkey's identity – and, long ago, I always feared falling foul of the military. However, much has changed. If only this book had been around then I would have met Turks to discuss these things with.

Sevan and Müjde have devoted themselves for many years to unearthing the best of Turkey to show visitors. And you could kick off your stay with a visit to their hotel: it is among the best of this bunch. Sevan laments, as we do, the ravages of modern tourism. He is passionate about Turkish history and heritage. He hugely enjoys people and is able to get the best out of them. His selection of places to stay is just as our own would have been: places of quirkiness, comfort, architectural interest and beauty. Above all, he is ready to introduce you to some fascinating people.

Via these pages you will learn of a Turkey that has far more to show you than you dare hope. Be bold, and venture deep. You will be richly rewarded.

Alastair Sawday

Introduction

WHAT COUNTS, FOR US, ARE PEOPLE, ARCHITECTURE, HISTORY, VIEWS AND, ABOVE ALL, ATMOSPHERE.

A meeting of hearts
The Little Hotel Book has been published in Turkey annually since 1998. Each one of its eight editions has been a national bestseller.
It has been hailed as a pioneer of alternative tourism and credited with initiating the country-wide trend for small hotels of character and charm.

At heart, it remains a very modest enterprise: a collection of hotels that we, a husband-and-wife team who enjoy travelling, happen to like very much. We like hotels with a personality – a 'soul', so to speak. So we give wide berth to properties that are run by impersonal managing companies or cater mainly to the package trade. We admire designer's pluck as an alternative to mediocrity, though we are often happier with a comfortable old armchair.

And we limit ourselves to small hotels. Having – regrettably – outgrown our own backpacking days, we insist on a certain standard of comfort and quality. We never lose sight of the luxuries that really count: a clean bed, a hot bath, a bottle of good wine.

Imagine our delight when we discovered Alastair Sawday's Special Places, which describes itself in the following terms:
'These books are founded upon a passion for the unpretentious, the genuine and the unique. Our criteria for deciding whether a place is special may appear obscure – we have no 'star' system and do not include somewhere just because it has all the right 'facilities'. What counts, for us, are people, architecture, history, views and, above all, atmosphere. A faded 17th century palace run by a generous, spirited family would be chosen in preference over a slick, designer hotel with all the five-star trimmings but surly staff.'

We met in Bristol, then in Şirince. We confirmed that we spoke the same language. The book was reviewed and adapted for an

Photos Nişanyan Gezi Tanitim Ltd

Introduction

English-speaking readership. Some hotels were dropped and others added. Facts were re-checked and brought into line with ASP specs. Thus was *Special Places to Stay – Turkey* born.

Unexpected Turkish delights

Turkey is always a surprise to the first-time visitor. Nearly everything you thought you knew about this vast and dynamic country turns out to be less than certain on closer inspection. The landscape is fantastically varied. The historic sites impress even the most un-historically minded. The people never cease to amaze by their spontaneous charm and innate generosity. Everywhere you meet people who are willing to bend rules, or risk their own comfort, just to please a visitor – though he or she might be a perfect stranger to them.

Tourism has of course wrought some damage; 17 million visited the country in 2004 alone, and that number grows by more than 10 percent a year. In its wake come the usual ills of mass travel – crowded beaches, standardised amenities, much gloss, and a boomtown mentality that infects and rots the attitudes of otherwise nice people.

This book argues that all is yet far from lost. The best part of Turkey remains mostly uninfected. To find it, you have to step a little away from the beaten path. You will discover a country that is friendly, relaxed, civilised and refreshingly free from the soul–numbing stereotypes of packaged tourism.

Start with a map

The great majority of travellers to Turkey pen themselves into three areas. First, the great city of Istanbul. Second, the south-western coast between Izmir and Antalya, full of sea resorts and sunny Mediterranean landscapes. Third, the fantastic region of Cappadocia in the interior. The rest of the country remains *terra incognita* for all practical purposes. Two vastly interesting areas, the far eastern coast of the Black Sea and the deep south-east, receive a trickle of pioneers. The north-western interior, a region of well-preserved historic towns, is just beginning to wake up to its visitor potential. The soft-hued northern Aegean is popular with Turkish families on summer holidays, but sees less than a tenth of the international crowds flocking to the sunnier south.

As an unfailing rule, your likelihood of falling in love with Turkey is proportional to how far away you travel from the usual tourist destinations. Nearly every town and village in the country holds something of interest for the curious visitor, and the people actually seem to like meeting you once you extricate yourself from the crowds. Security is not a problem. There are decent, if usually unexciting, places to stay nearly everywhere in the country.

Having said this, however, it remains true that the really interesting, attractive and memorable hotels tend to be where the tourists go. A majority of the properties in this guide, too, are crowded into the three main tourist areas. We have made a brave effort to spread our coverage; we have even lowered our criteria a little bit in order to include a few entries from the mountains of the Black Sea and the ancient towns of the Mesopotamian plain. The locations are often so magnificent, one forgives the occasional plastic chair or unkempt garden.

The authors
Sevan & Müjde Nişanyan live in Şirince, a delightful village in the hills of Aegean Turkey, near Ephesus, with their three children and various other dependents. They have a small hotel of their own, which they have ventured to include in this volume.

Sevan & Müjde Nişanyan

Introduction

Photo Turkish Culture & Tourism Office

How to use this book
Prices

Being special has little to do with price. Our selection, accordingly, ranges from hundreds of pounds at the top end to less than £15 at the bottom. The median price for a two-bed room, with breakfast, during the summer high season lies around £45. This is somewhat higher than the Turkish average, but still cheaper than the rest of the Mediterranean. There is usually a straightforward correlation between price and the level of 'class' and luxury provided. An exception to the rule is the Bodrum peninsula, the summer home of Turkey's fashionable classes, where you are expected to pay in summer twice as much as a comparable hotel elsewhere on the Turkish coast. Istanbul is relatively expensive, too, whereas in the humble northeast £20 is still considered an outrageous price to charge a guest for a comfortable room and a good breakfast.

Turkish hotels quote their prices in euros, dollars, Turkish lira or, very occasionally, in pounds sterling. We have converted all into the new Turkish lira (YTL, short for Yeni Türk Lirası), using the exchange rates at the time of going to press (May 2005), and then rounding slightly. Our figures should be taken to give a general indication only: it is essential to check before booking to avoid surprises. You must also keep in mind that much can change in the course of the two-year lifespan of this edition, particularly in a country as dynamic as Turkey.

Prices reflect **high season rates**, which are typically valid from July to mid-September. Rates at other times are usually, though not always, lower by 10 to 30 percent. Unless otherwise specified, all prices apply to **a double or twin room**, or to two persons in an apartment or house. The same is valid for half-board. Single prices generally refer to single occupancy of a double room. Breakfast is included, unless we say otherwise.

Most hotels will be happy to offer a 5 or 10 percent discount on cash payment; others prefer to add a premium on credit card payment (VAT in Turkey is at 18%), though this will be announced in advance. Haggling on prices may yield some result if you show up late on the day and there are empty beds to fill. It is unlikely to be very effective otherwise.

Types of properties

More than half of the properties in this guide are **hotels** in the proper sense of the term, with a reception area and a lobby, usually a restaurant, and round-the-clock attendance. Some prefer to call themselves 'boutique hotels'. Nearly all of them are less than 15 years old, though some occupy historic houses several hundred years old.

Guest houses are harder to define. The basic difference may be that there isn't a properly defined reception – and you may feel the urge to address the proprietor by his or her first name. A guest house is usually called a *pension* or *pansiyon*, though the Turkish term *konukevi* (literally, 'guest house') is becoming more widespread. True pensions, or B&Bs, consisting of a few rooms in somebody's house, have become a rarity in Turkey. We include none in this guide, as we find the existing ones either too modest or unstable.

Self-catering flats, or 'apartments', are all the rage in the south-western resorts. Typically they appeal to the budget end of mass tourism, and accordingly we have found only a handful that break the general mould sufficiently to qualify as a Special Place. Self-catering cottages, or holiday homes, by contrast, tend to include many houses of extraordinary charm and character. We quote the daily rate only, so check with the owners about possible minimum stays.

Finally we have several **camps**, including a couple of yoga and meditation set-ups, which we have

Photo Nişanyan Gezi Tanitim Ltd

Introduction

selected for their unforgettable location and natural environment. In each case they have some sort of fixed accommodation to offer – from cabins to tree houses – in addition to tent space.

A **bungalow** in Turkish usage means what you would ordinarily call a cabin in England: a purpose-made unit of, usually, wood or brick, often deployed in series. Quite a few establishments in the warmer south consist of clusters of 'bungalows' – employed in most cases to bypass building regulations. The natural setting sometimes compensates for the lack of architectural interest.

Bedrooms, bathrooms, etc.
Over 90 percent of hotels covered here, like the great majority of

Turkish hotels in general, have bedrooms with en suite bathrooms. This should be understood to be the case unless we say otherwise. A shower is standard, baths are rarer. Old-style Turkish squat loos have all but disappeared from hotels: only one of our entries still sports one. An adaptor plug is useful to have if you are carrying English electrical equipment along. Heating is a factor to bear in mind if you are travelling off-season: a cold April night on the Mediterranean or Aegean coast, where most hotels are built with summer conditions in mind, can be an unpleasant experience.

Meals
Turkish food is varied, interesting, invariably tasty, and usually cheap. Contrary to received opinion, it is not spicy at all except in the case of some south-eastern regional specialties. Non-meat dishes form an integral part of the diet and are available everywhere.

A traditional restaurant meal involves several rounds of cold and warm appetisers (meze) followed by a main course, usually of simply grilled fish or meat. More fashionable now in the classier restaurants of Western Turkey is so-called Mediterranean or Aegean cuisine – classic Turkish dishes prepared with lots of olive oil and fresh herbs, with a little French flair or Greek colour added to taste. Rakı, a potent anise-flavoured spirit, is the usual accompaniment to the former. Wine is the obvious choice for the latter.

Most of our hotels feature excellent restaurants of their own; a few will provide a home-cooked dinner on request. We quote an approximate price for dinner, for one person, with a glass of rakı or a half-bottle of wine, to give you a general idea only. When a hotel does not provide dinner, it invariably means there are plenty of restaurants within walking distance.

Closing dates

Annual opening and closing dates are remarkably flexible in the case of small and family-run hotels and may depend on day-to-day decisions. As a rule of thumb the season runs from mid-end April through to October along the southern coast and in Cappadocia, and from May to September in the Northern Aegean. Istanbul hotels do not normally close.

Our closing dates are based on what the hotel keepers told us: there is no guarantee that they will hold true a year from now. Some hotels that are technically closed in winter may be willing to admit guests by prior reservation. Others run on reduced staff, or may shut

down for short breaks. The phrase **'partly closed in winter'** means: phone in advance to make sure.

Booking

Over 80 percent of the properties in this guide have an email address and use it more or less regularly. For the rest you may use the telephone. Better still, you can use the online services of *www.nisanyan.net* to place reservations.

In mid-summer you are unlikely to find a room near the Aegean and Mediterranean shores unless you act at least a month or two in advance. Things are more relaxed during the rest of the year. A credit card guarantee is usually required, on the understanding that either

Photos Nişanyan Gezi Tanitim Ltd

Introduction

half or all of the reservation cost will be charged in the event of a last-minute cancellation. Reconfirming your reservation a few days in advance is always a good idea.

Getting others to do it for you
Argonaut Escapades, a small travel agency based in Ürgüp (Cappadocia) and Selçuk (Aegean region), has specialised over the years in working with the hotels listed in this book. They will make your bookings, arrange your transportation, provide expert advice and organise tours for you. You can contact Argonaut Escapades at www.argonautturkey.com

Quick reference indices
At the back of the book is a quick reference section to help direct you to the places that suit you, be they equipped for wheelchair users, places with outside space for lounging with a book or those just a short stroll from a beach.

Subscriptions
Owners pay to appear in this guide. Their fee goes towards the high costs of inspecting and producing an all-colour book. We only include places that we like and find special for one reason or another, so it is **NOT** possible to buy – or bribe! – your way in.

Disclaimer
We do not claim to be purely objective in choosing our *Special Places*. They are here because we, and our inspectors and editors, like them. Our opinions and our tastes are ours alone and this book is a statement of them; we hope that you share them.

We try hard to get our facts right, but if any glaring errors have crept in then we apologise. If you are burning to tell us of any flaws or inaccuracies then do write to us. We welcome feedback and act on it.

Internet
www.specialplacestostay.com has online pages for all the special places featured here and from all our other books – around 4,500 places to stay in total. There are a searchable database, a snippet of the write-up and colour photos. New kid on the block is our dedicated British holiday homes web site *www.special-escapes.co.uk*

And finally
We love your letters and value your comments; they make a real contribution to our guides, be they on our report form, by letter or by email to info@sawdays.co.uk. You can also visit our web site and write to us from there.

General Map

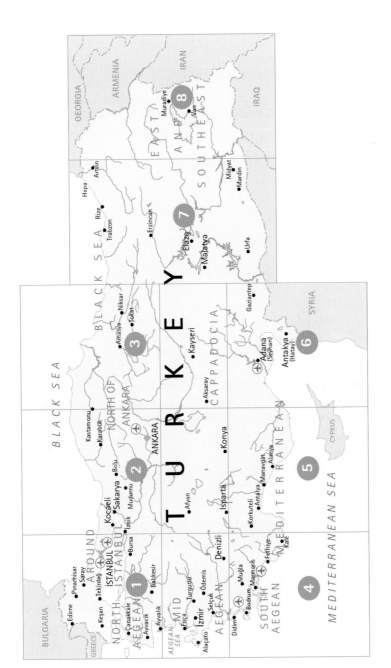

©Maidenhead Cartographic, 2005

Map 1

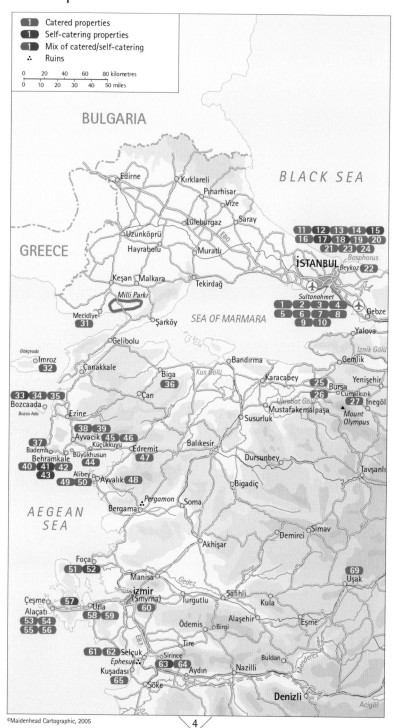

Catered properties
Self-catering properties
Mix of catered/self-catering
∴ Ruins

0 20 40 60 80 kilometres
0 10 20 30 40 50 miles

BULGARIA

BLACK SEA

Edirne Kırklareli
Pınarhisar
Vize
Lüleburgaz Saray

GREECE

Uzunköprü
Hayrabolu Muratlı
Keşan Malkara Tekirdağ
Milli Parkı
Mecidiye
31 Şarköy SEA OF MARMARA

11 12 13 14 15
16 17 18 19 20
21 23 24
İSTANBUL Beykoz 22
Bosphorus

Sultanahmet
1 2 3 4
5 6 7 8
9 10
Gebze
Yalova

İznik Gölü

Gökçeada
Imroz
32
Gelibolu
Çanakkale
Biga
Can
Kus Gölü
Bandırma
Karacabey
25
26
Bursa
Cumalıkızık
27 İnegöl
Gemlik
Yenişehir

33 34 35
Bozcaada
Bozca Ada
Ezine
38 39
Ayvacık 45 46
Küçükkuyu
Büyükhusun
44
Edremit
47
Balıkesir
Mustafakemálpaşa
Susurluk
Uluabat Gölü
Mount
Olympus
36

37
Bademli
Behramkale
40 41 42
43 Alibey
49 50 Ayvalık 48
Pergamon
Bergama
Soma
Dursunbey
Bigadiç
Tavşanlı

AEGEAN
SEA

Demirci Simav

Akhisar

Foça
51 52

Manisa
Gedez
İzmir
(Smyrna)
60
Turgutlu
Salihli
Kula
Uşak
69

Çeşme 57
Alaçatı Urla
53 54 58 59
55 56
Ödemiş Birgi
Alaşehir
Eşme
Tire

61 62 Selçuk
Ephesus ∴ Sirince
63 64
Kuşadası
65 Söke
Aydın Nazilli
Buldan
Menderes
Denizli
Acıgöl

Map 2

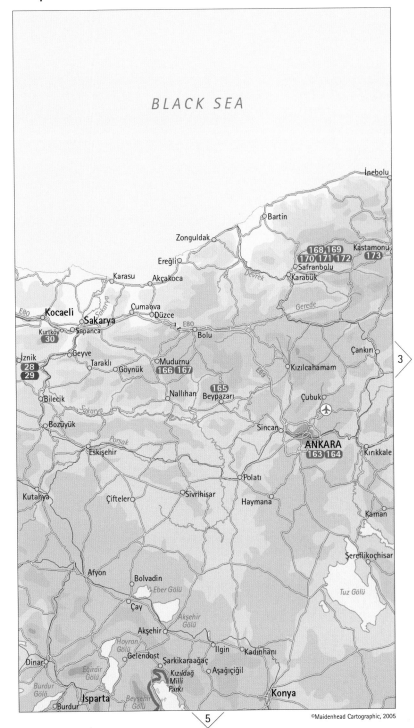

Map 3

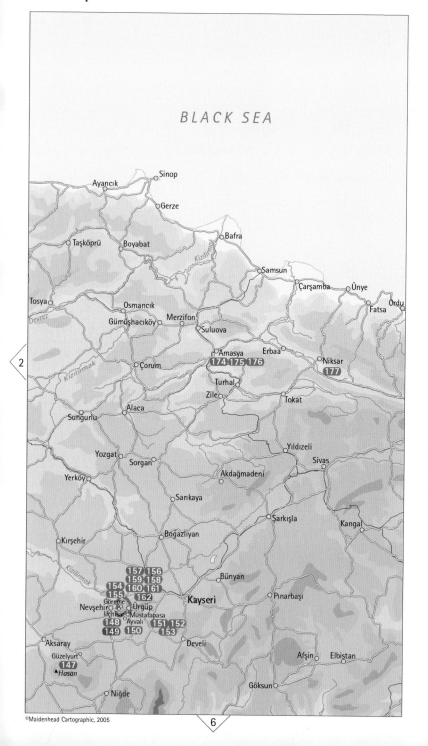

BLACK SEA

Ayancık Sinop

Gerze

Taşköprü Boyabat Bafra

Kızıl...

Samsun Çarşamba Ünye

Tosya Osmancık Ordu

Devrez Gümüshacıköy Merzifon Fatsa

Suluova

Amasya Erbaa

2 Çorum **174 175 176** Niksar

177

Turhal

Zile Tokat

Kızılırmak

Alaca

Sungurlu

Yıldızeli

Yozgat Sivas

Sorgan

Yerköy Akdağmadeni

Sarıkaya

Şarkışla Kangal

Kırşehir Boğazlıyan

Kızılırmak

157 156 Bünyan

159 158

154 160 161

155 162

Göreme **Kayseri** Pınarbaşı

Nevşehir Ürgüp

Uchisar Mustafapasa

148 Ayvalı **151 152**

149 150 **153**

Aksaray Develi

Güzelyurt

147 Afşin Elbistan

▲*Hasan*

Niğde Göksun

Map 4

23

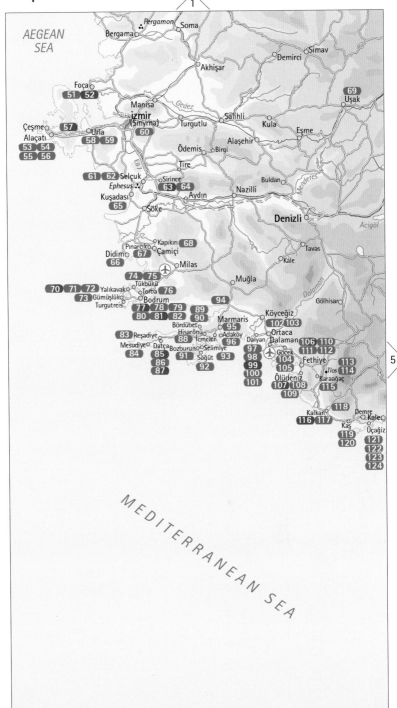

Map 5

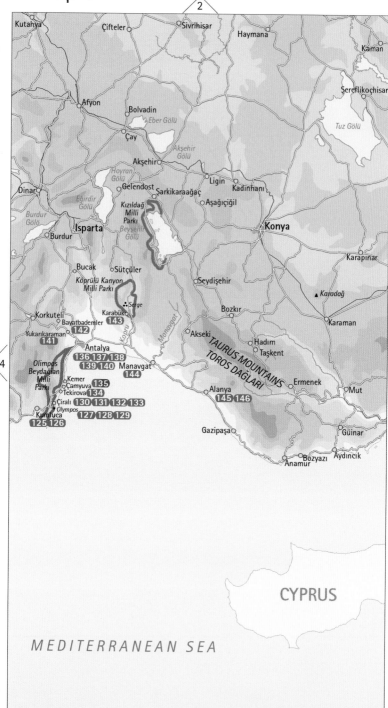

Map 6

25

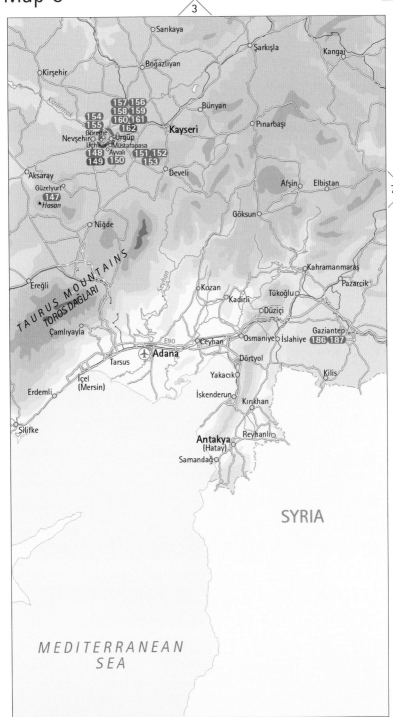

Map 7

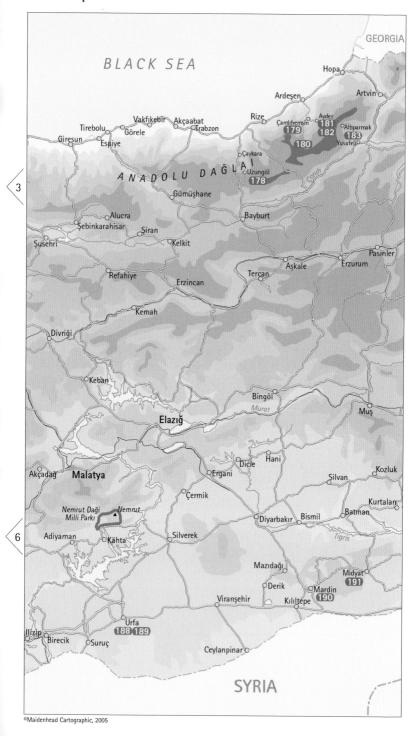

Map 8

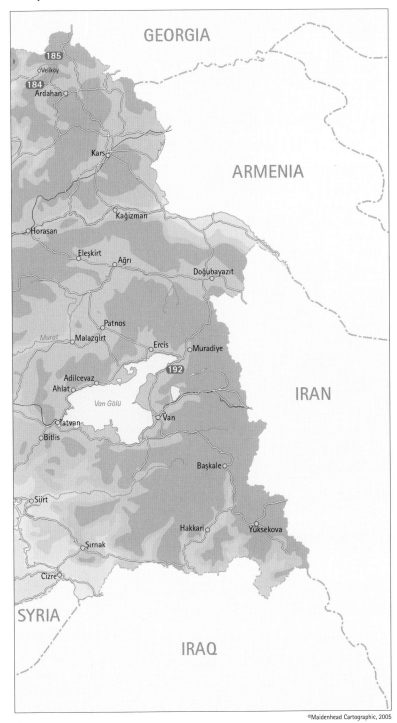

GEORGIA

185
Veliköy
184
Ardahan

Kars

ARMENIA

Kağizman

Horasan

Eleşkirt
Ağrı

Doğubayazıt

Patnos
Murat Malazgirt
Ercis
Muradiye

Adilcevaz
Ahlat
192
Van Gölü
Tatvan
Van

IRAN

Bitlis

Başkale

Siirt

Hakkari
Yüksekova

Şırnak

Cizre

SYRIA

IRAQ

©Maidenhead Cartographic, 2005

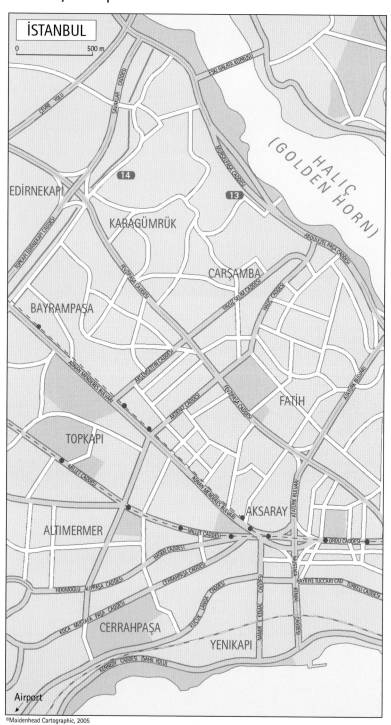

İSTANBUL

0   500 m

HALİÇ (İGOLDEN HORN)

EDİRNEKAPI

KARAGÜMRÜK

CARŞAMBA

BAYRAMPAŞA

FATİH

TOPKAPI

AKSARAY

ALTIMERMER

MILLET CADDESI

CERRAHPAŞA

YENIKAPI

Airport

©Maidenhead Cartographic, 2005

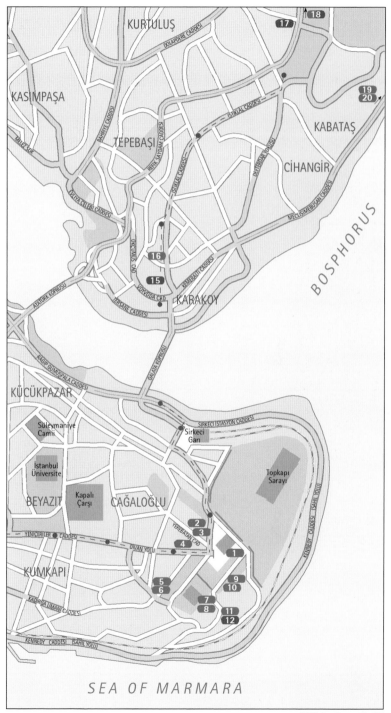

©Maidenhead Cartographic, 2005

City maps

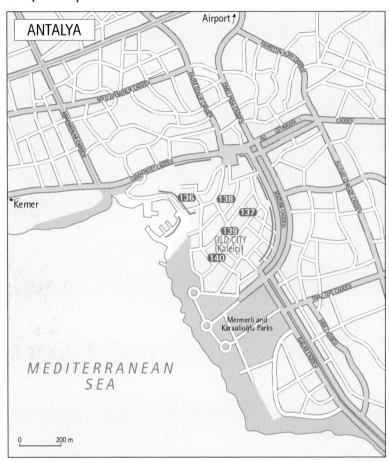

ANTALYA

Airport ↑

Kemer

136   138

137

139

OLD CITY
(Kaleiçi)

140

Mermerli and
Karaalioğlu Parks

MEDITERRANEAN
SEA

0   200 m

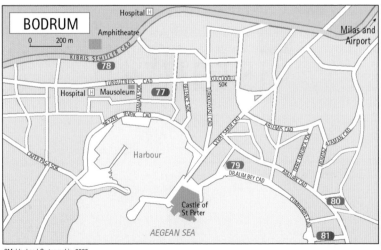

BODRUM

Hospital Ⓗ

Amphitheatre

0   200 m

Milas and
Airport

KIBRIS ŞEHİTLER CAD

78

TURGUTREIS CAD

Hospital Ⓗ   Mausoleum

77

Harbour

79

DR ALIM BEY CAD

80

Castle of
St Peter

81

AEGEAN SEA

©Maidenhead Cartographic, 2005

Photo Turkish Culture & Tourism Office

istanbul

istanbul:
metropolis of the east

Tourists' Istanbul is centred on Sultanahmet Square. The great monuments of two empires — the Hagia Sophia, Blue Mosque and Topkapı Palace along with a host of lesser marvels — cluster here next to a colourful melée of cafés, small hotels, carpet shops and antique dealers. Twenty years ago this used to be no-man's land; now it is a pleasant and increasingly sophisticated district with a small-town feel and little traffic. The bazaar is a short walk away; Eminönü, the transport hub of Istanbul, a quick hop down the hill.

The modern heart of the city beats on the other side of the Haliç — the bay also known as the Golden Horn. İstiklal Street and the warren of 19th-century alleys branching from it are where the crowds go for an evening stroll, but for sophisticated shopping and dining you should venture further north to the fashionable districts of Nişantaşı, Etiler, Levent and Maslak.

The 'villages' along both banks of the Bosphorus were the summer playgrounds of the Ottoman ruling classes; they remain the most civilised places to live in the city. The recent trend to convert old Bosphorus palaces and stately waterfront homes into luxury hotels has yielded three or four notable results.

Ayasofya Houses

Soğukçeşme Sok., Sultanahmet, 34122 Istanbul

No other hotel in Istanbul can convey its historic character quite as forcefully. This picturesque lane of old houses squeezed between the city's two greatest imperial monuments – Hagia Sophia and the Topkapı Palace – was revived as a hotel complex in the 1980s by the Touring Club of Turkey. Built against the outer Palace wall, these gaily-painted houses hold four or five hotel rooms each. A bigger, four-storey mansion set in its own garden is a separate option. They are all elegantly furnished in the gilded quasi-European style favoured by the Ottoman elite of the late 19th century: tassels, pelmets, curlicues and comfort. An underground cistern of Roman origin, if not earlier, serves as one of three restaurants, there's a research library devoted to the history of Istanbul and the cobbled street is closed to motor traffic: you take a real step back in time. In early 2005, long-overdue renovation restored the Ayasofya Houses to their rightful standing as one of the finest – as well as the most atmospheric – of Istanbul's top-range hotels.

rooms	63: 57 twins/doubles, 6 suites.
price	160 YTL. Suites 250 YTL. Singles from 120 YTL.
meals	30-45 YTL, with wine.
closed	Never.
directions	In Sultanahmet: between Hagia Sophia and Topkapi Palace main gate.
airport	18km from Istanbul Airport.

	Aykut Bakay
tel	+90 (212) 5133660
fax	+90 (212) 5133669
email	info@ayasofyapensions.com
web	www.ayasofyapensions.com

Hotel

Map 1 / City Map p29   Entry 1

Kybele Hotel

Yerebatan Cad. 35, Sultanahmet, 34110 Istanbul

Ali Baba's treasure house? Istanbul townhouse? Hotel? Whatever the definition, this is a fantastic menagerie of oriental kilims, antique armchairs, calligraphic plates, bronze candle-holders, old Turkish door panels and a piano, all stuffed into the maze-like recesses of two historic townhouses. The lobby is lit by one thousand and two individually crafted lamps of antique glass — one better than those proverbial nights. Best of all, the Kybele has grown organically and the slick touch of the designer is nowhere to be felt. The owners are three marvellously smooth brothers whose collective biography includes many years of dealing in antiques and carpets, an engineering degree, an officer's commission with the Turkish army and three years' experience in an Australian circus. They speak English and Japanese and several other languages fluently, play a mighty backgammon and are disarmingly gallant towards their guests. Under the ground is the Yerebatan Cistern, a 6th-century subterranean reservoir held aloft by more than 300 marble columns. What more could you want?

rooms	18: 16 twins/doubles, 2 suites.
price	160 YTL. Suites 210 YTL. Singles 100 YTL.
meals	Restaurants nearby.
closed	Never.
directions	In Sultanahmet: near Yerebatan Cistern.
airport	18km from Istanbul Airport.

	Hasan, Alp, 'Mike' Akbayrak
tel	+90 (212) 5117766
fax	+90 (212) 5134393
email	info@kybelehotel.com
web	www.kybelehotel.com

Hotel

Celal Sultan Hotel

Yerebatan Cad. Salkımsöğüt Sok. 16, Sultanahmet, 34410 Istanbul

With its deft combination of classic comfort and modern finish, this stylish townhouse-hotel would look perfectly at home in the elegant streets of any decent western European city. The hospitality, however, is unmistakably Turkish in its spontaneous charm. The hosts run the hotel in a friendly and attentive manner and load their guests with helpful sightseeing and shopping tips; at the end of an exhausting day about the city, you will be tempted to share your impressions with Ms Selami over a cup of coffee in her cramped little office. The location is a quiet lane behind Hagia Sophia, right above the fantastic thousand-columned cisterns of ancient Byzantium. The historic house has been renovated in restrained taste and decorated with a wealth of curios from the *belle époque* of late-Ottoman Istanbul. Rooms are in pristine condition, lovely kilims bring ancient colours to new warm hardwood floors and pale softness glows. And you can make intimate eye-to-eye contact with Hagia Sophia over breakfast on the roof terrace.

rooms	30: 28 twins/doubles, 2 suites.
price	150–200 YTL. Suites 260 YTL. Singles from 110 YTL.
meals	45-60 YTL, with wine.
closed	Never.
directions	In Sultanahmet: beside Yerebatan Cistern, opposite Hagia Sophia.
airport	18km from Istanbul Airport.

	Şule & Emir Selami
tel	+90 (212) 5209323
fax	+90 (212) 5229724
email	info@celalsultan.com
web	www.celalsultan.com

Hotel

Map 1 / City Map p29 Entry 3

Nomade Hotel

Divanyolu Ticarethane Sok. 15, Sultanahmet, 34400 Istanbul

One of the oldest among the townhouse-hotels in Istanbul's historic Sultanahmet district, Nomade has a loyal clientele that includes journalists, academics and interesting people of all nationalities. The atmosphere of easygoing hospitality owes much to the twin sisters Esra and Hamra who own and run the hotel: French-educated, widely-travelled and fluent in several languages, they support their guests wholeheartedly in all matters from travelling tips to shopping advice. Indeed, the *Lonely Planet* commends Nomade as "a good place for single women travellers." The hotel underwent a thorough renovation in 2004, shedding the last traces of its post-60s youth in the process. The rooms, each one furnished in a different colour scheme, are simple, bright, contemporary and chic. From the inviting roof terrace, where dinner tables are stylishly dressed, you can feast upon a sweeping panorama of Istanbul's great monuments. Also part of the hotel is Rumeli Café across the street, probably the best café-bistro in the historic part of the city.

rooms	16: 13 twins/doubles, 3 suites.
price	130 YTL. Suites 160 YTL. Singles 100 YTL.
meals	30-45 YTL, with wine.
closed	Never.
directions	In Sultanahmet: first right on Divanyolu Avenue.
airport	18km from Istanbul Airport.

	Esra & Hamra Teker
tel	+90 (212) 5111296
fax	+90 (212) 5132404
email	info@hotelnomade.com
web	www.hotelnomade.com

Hotel

İbrahim Pasha Hotel

Terzihane Sok. 5, Sultanahmet, 34400 Istanbul

The Ibrahim Pasha is a civilised small hotel that stands out among the welter of happy-go-lucky little sleeping places in the Sultanahmet area by virtue of its innate sense of style and friendly staff. Don't expect turbaned pashas in this renovated 19th-century townhouse: the atmosphere is restrained and European with a touch of neo-classical and a hint of 1920s Paris. A magnificent Corinthian capital (genuine, Roman) supports the massive glass reception desk; a log-burning fireplace enlivens the small lobby. Bedrooms are colourful and contemporary if rather small – with the exception of one well-endowed suite – and have all you'd expect for the price. In 2005, an in-depth renovation upgraded the furniture and the infrastructure. The roof terrace opens out to a breathtaking close-up of the Blue Mosque and the Egyptian obelisk. Across the street, the many-domed palace of Ibrahim Pasha, now the Museum of Turkish and Islamic Arts, houses superb collections of illuminated Turkish manuscripts, Islamic calligraphy and antique carpets. Don't miss it.

rooms	16: 12 twins/doubles, 4 suites.
price	160 YTL. Suites 230 YTL. Singles 140 YTL.
meals	Restaurants nearby.
closed	Never.
directions	In Sultanahmet: off south-west corner of the Hippodrome near Turkish-Islamic Arts Museum.
airport	18km from Istanbul Airport.

	Mehmet Umur
tel	+90 (212) 5180394
fax	+90 (212) 5184457
email	contact@ibrahimpasha.com
web	www.ibrahimpasha.com

Hotel

Map 1/City Map p29 Entry 5

Alzer Hotel

At Meydanı 72, Sultanahmet, 34400 Istanbul

A friendly mom-and-pop hotel set right in the middle of Istanbul's great imperial monuments. The city's crowning glory, the Blue Mosque, is across the street, the palace of the Grand Vizier is next door and just where you casually pull up your café table is where the Hippodrome factions used to raise hell against the Byzantine emperors. The Alzer may be nothing much to look at from the outside but inside the rooms are big and charmingly furnished. The 1,000 square-foot Pasha's room would do honour to the Grand Vizier himself and a breathtakingly panoramic roof terrace doubles up as breakfast hall. The main attraction, however, is the human element. The Sur family runs the hotel with the sort of earnest hospitality that one takes for granted in a remote country inn but would hardly expect in the heart of the metropolis. After more than ten years in business, they still seem to care, genuinely care. The guest book glows with testimonies to this homey haven, far from the raucous tribulations of the city.

rooms	21 twins/doubles.
price	120-160 YTL. Singles from 100 YTL.
meals	30-45 YTL, with wine.
closed	Never.
directions	In Sultanahmet: in south-west corner of the Hippodrome.
airport	18km from Istanbul Airport.

	Aysen & Metin Sur
tel	+90 (212) 5166262
fax	+90 (212) 5160000
email	alzer@alzerhotel.com
web	www.alzerhotel.com

Hotel

Map 1 / City Map p29   Entry 6

Ararat Hotel

Torun Sok. 3, Sultanahmet, 34400 Istanbul

An intimate, friendly and artistic hotel right next to the Blue Mosque, the Ararat manages to be low-budget and low-key without showing too many barbs for it. The rooms are fashioned in warm colours and decorated with unusual Byzantine-style murals by a talented Greek artist; beds are dressed in crisp white linen. Some bedrooms are rather cramped; others are reasonably comfortable and you pay more for a room with a view; our favourites are the two tiny ones on the top floor which are reached through the loft common room. If you are lucky enough to witness the other guests leaving early in the evening, this will turn into a delightful private sitting room – overwhelmed by the illuminated domes of the Blue Mosque that towers across the street. On the other side, you can watch the sun set across a broad and beautiful view, over the Sea of Marmara as far as the Prince's Islands. Another great asset is Haydar himself, your suave and charismatic host: he adds an intelligent personal touch that is so often lacking in the average visitor's experience of the big city.

rooms	13: 12 twins/doubles, 1 suite.
price	100-135 YTL. Suite 160 YTL. Singles from 100 YTL.
meals	Restaurants nearby.
closed	Never.
directions	In Sultanahmet: behind the Blue Mosque.
airport	18km from Istanbul Airport.

	Haydar Sarıgül
tel	+90 (212) 5160411
fax	+90 (212) 5185241
email	info@ararathotel.com
web	www.ararathotel.com

Hotel

Map 1/City Map p29 Entry 7

Sultanahmet Palace Hotel

Torun Sok. 19, Sultanahmet, 34400 Istanbul

The Great Palace of Constantine used to stand on this spot. Indeed, a mosaic floor belonging to the palace was discovered some years ago four metres below street level and turned into a museum. The Blue Mosque – Sultanahmet Camii to Turks – with its breathtaking cascade of domes, rises right in front of the hotel. The rear view reigns over the Bosphorus – and two continents. One could scarcely imagine a more grandiose position on earth. The hotel itself is quite as grand. The style – post-Victorian pseudo-Ottoman neo-Baroque – may strike purists as a bit overdone, but who could mind spending a few days in the lap of such wonderfully unabashed luxury? Or resist the sinful comfort of a private marble-inlaid Turkish bath, albeit tiny, attached to one's room – a luxury matched by no other hotel in this book? The staff will give you quiet, courteous service and the gardens come as a welcome relief in the cramped historic quarters of the city.

rooms	36 twins/doubles.
price	200-300 YTL. Singles from 170 YTL.
meals	30-45 YTL, with wine.
closed	Never.
directions	In Sultanahmet: behind the Blue Mosque.
airport	18km from Istanbul Airport.

	Şükrü Barutçu
tel	+90 (212) 4580460
fax	+90 (212) 5186224
email	saray@sultanahmetpalace.com
web	www.sultanahmetpalace.com

Hotel

Map 1 / City Map p29   Entry 8

Yeşil Ev

Kabasakal Cad. 5, Sultanahmet, 34122 Istanbul

Turkey used to be an empire before it became something else, and it used to have an aristocracy, though you'll meet few traces of that lost breed now. Set quietly off the park near the former Imperial Palace, Yeşil Ev (the Green House) is the well-preserved townhouse of one of those aristocrats. Some rooms are furnished with the personal effects of Reşid Saffet, a celebrated dandy of the last days of the empire who survived into the 1950s as chairman of the Touring Club; some of the staff, too, seem to date back to the time of servants and eunuchs. Recent renovation has managed to modernise the facilities without touching the strangely self-effacing atmosphere that is reticent rather than boastful, despite the tasselled velvet curtains, brass bedsteads, chandeliers and all. President Mitterrand of France and Queen Sophia of Spain, among others, seem to have enjoyed it. The conservatory, where breakfast is now served, hails straight from a Proustian *temps perdu*. The walled garden, smothered in ivy, has a great fountain of pink porphyry at its heart; the dome of Hagia Sophia peeks over the wall.

rooms	19: 18 twins/doubles, 1 suite.
price	220 YTL. Suite 350 YTL. Singles 160 YTL.
meals	30-45 YTL, with wine.
closed	Never.
directions	In Sultanahmet: between Blue Mosque & Hagia Sophia.
airport	18km from Istanbul Airport.

	Nesrin Özkök
tel	+90 (212) 5176785
fax	+90 (212) 5176780
email	info@istanbulyesilev.com
web	www.istanbulyesilev.com

Hotel

Empress Zoe Hotel

Akbıyık Cad. Adliye Sok. 10, Sultanahmet, 34400 Istanbul

An attractively designed small hotel that is at once friendly and unpretentious, yet impeccable in its details. Ann, the owner, is a former resident of San Francisco who first came to Sultanahmet in 1989 and never got around to leaving. The hotel occupies two old townhouses in the heart of tourist Istanbul. The main building is the child of a younger and less ambitious Ann: it is somewhat cramped inside, with a minaret-style staircase that may prove a challenge to the less agile. The second house, full of skilfully re-used historic textures and beautiful objects, is a marvel of tasteful styling in a limited space. Each of its four suites has its own Turkish bath in genuine Marmara marble. Joining the two houses is a wonderful garden – a little gem that incorporates the ruin of a 15th-century bathhouse to immensely romantic effect. Down below, an Ottoman – or possibly Byzantine – cistern lurks under the lobby; right at the top, a deck terrace commands the usual grand views of the monuments and the sea.

rooms	22: 14 twins/doubles, 8 suites.
price	150 YTL. Suites 190-260 YTL. Singles from 110 YTL.
meals	Restaurants nearby.
closed	Never.
directions	In Sultanahmet: behind the Four Seasons Hotel.
airport	18km from Istanbul Airport.

	Ann Nevans
tel	+90 (212) 5182504
fax	+90 (212) 5185699
email	info@emzoe.com
web	www.emzoe.com

Hotel

Armada Hotel

Ahırkapı Sok. 24, Cankurtaran, 34122 Istanbul

The Armada is not small, but it is so special in spirit and personality that we do not hesitate to include it with the best hotels *of human scale* in Turkey. It has local character without any of the usual tourist tinsel and it offers the amenities and comforts of a large cosmopolitan hotel without the chill smugness of most of those institutions. By the second day you'll know the waiters by name; next, you begin bonding with the turtles in the lobby pool. The neighbourhood is an asset. It is a modest residential backwater with friendly local restaurants and chatty local grocers, yet it is within strolling distance of the monumental hub of the Old City. The entertainment is often brilliant: the most stylish legs of Istanbul congregate at the Armada twice a week for tango nights; the neighbourhood gypsy band grew to international fame under the hotel's auspices; the roof restaurant, which has a glorious view of the harbour, serves first-rate cuisine in the Istanbul tradition. The best rooms are the 'corner' rooms with views.

rooms	110 twins/doubles.
price	120-230 YTL. Singles from 100 YTL.
meals	From 50 YTL, with wine.
closed	Never.
directions	1km from Eminönü: seafront drive, first right after Ahırkapı lighthouse, one block in.
airport	18km from Istanbul Airport.

	Kasım Zoto
tel	+90 (212) 4554455
fax	+90 (212) 4554496
email	info@armadahotel.com.tr
web	www.armadahotel.com.tr

Hotel

Map 1/City Map p29 Entry 11

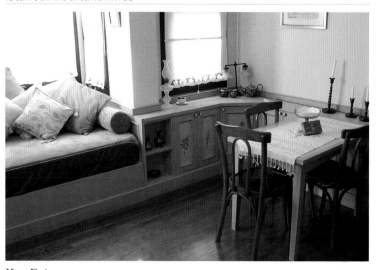

Kuş Evi

Yenigüvey Sok. 3, Ahırkapı, 34122 Istanbul

Kuş Evi, an old Istanbul house attractively converted into three self-catering flats, is English owned – and furnished with considerable charm. The flats are offered for rent through Armada Hotel, the friendliest of Istanbul's larger hotels, which is just round the corner (see opposite). For the short-term visitor, these flats offer the chance to enjoy Istanbul from the privacy of a comfortable home-from-home, while the facilities of a full-service hotel lie conveniently nearby. An extra bonus is the roof terrace: the view – with the Blue Mosque above, the harbour of Byzantium below – will haunt you for years. The position is as central as it gets, yet you can hardly find a quieter oasis in the city – the sort of place where the neighbours sit, Mediterranean-style, by their doorstep, and may just invite you over for some tea and gossip. If you don't wish to cook, there are several top-class restaurants within walking distance. The big monuments are a short jaunt up the hill and you can commute to the city's business centres by boat if you wish.

rooms	3 apartments for 2.
price	120 YTL. Breakfast extra.
meals	Restaurants nearby.
closed	Never.
directions	1km from Sultanahmet: behind the Armada Hotel.
airport	18km from Istanbul Airport.

	Mary Hall
tel	+90 (212) 6381370
fax	+90 (212) 5185060
email	info@armadahotel.com.tr

Self-catering

Map 1 / City Map p29   Entry 12

Daphnis Hotel

Sadrazam Ali Paşa Cad. 26, Fenerbahçe, 34220 Istanbul

A string of hundred-year-old townhouses, beautifully refurbished, stand in an old city district that seems caught in a time warp. Just down the street is the Greek Orthodox Patriarchate of Constantinople – the spiritual headquarters, in theory, of just about half of Christendom. Around it lie the desolate palaces of a long-forgotten plutocracy, serving as backdrop to a fantastically colourful slum. Until a few years ago, nobody ever came here; now, very slowly, the discoverers have gone to work. Ms Yanger, an architect in the other half of her life, is the creator and hands-on manager of this charming small hotel, the only one of its sort in this part of the city. The house is full of unexaggerated charm and loving detail, the service is personal yet unobtrusive and the five-o'clock cookies come fresh from the oven. Sitting in a grandmotherly chair in the bay window with a cup of Turkish coffee in hand, you may find even the Golden Horn looks romantic outside.

rooms	19: 16 twins/doubles, 3 suites.
price	90 YTL. Suites 130 YTL. Singles 70 YTL.
meals	20–30 YTL.
closed	Never.
directions	5km from Sultanahmet: on southern shore of Haliç, opposite Greek Patriarchat.
airport	13km from Istanbul Airport.

	Defne Yanger
tel	+90 (212) 5314858
fax	+90 (212) 5328992
email	info@hoteldaphnis.com
web	www.hoteldaphnis.com

Hotel

 Map 1/City Map p28 Entry 13

Kariye Hotel

Kariye Camii Sok. 18, Edirnekapı, 34240 Istanbul

In a charming old neighbourhood near the city walls, busy with gnome-sized wooden houses painted in candy colours and sidewalk cafés surrounding a traffic-free, cobble-stoned village square, the Kariye Hotel's position is like none other. In the centre of the square stands the Chora or Kariye, an 11th-century church, now converted into a museum, that is one of the world's most spectacular treasure houses of Byzantine art. It is a surprisingly isolated and quiet area, yet within easy reach – by taxi – of the city centre and the usual tourist haunts. The hotel occupies an attractive old mansion that was rebuilt by the Touring Club of Turkey and furnished in a somewhat dowdy but comfortable style. The rooms are light and remarkably quiet at night. The garden forms a calm and attractive oasis in summer, shaded as it is by tall chestnuts and linden trees. Its highly regarded restaurant, the Asitane, specialises in rare Ottoman dishes gleaned from old sources and original manuscripts.

rooms	27: 24 twins/doubles, 3 suites.
price	90-130 YTL. Suites 160 YTL. Singles from 80 YTL.
meals	45-60 YTL, with wine.
closed	Never.
directions	7km from Sultanahmet: inside west city wall beside Kariye/Chora museum.
airport	11km from Istanbul Airport.

	Güner Durmay
tel	+90 (212) 5348414
fax	+90 (212) 5216631
email	info@kariyeotel.com
web	www.kariyeotel.com

Hotel

Map 1 / City Map p28   Entry 14

Galata Residence

Bankalar Cad. Hacı Ali Sok., Galata, 34420 Istanbul

Galata Residence occupies the oldest apartment building in Istanbul – a brick pile built in 1881 for the renowned Jewish bankers, the Camondo family. The narrow lanes around it form a part of the city that is rarely seen by tourists: the historic district of Galata, once home to the city's Italian and Jewish communities. The Old City is a quick walk across the Galata Bridge, while an underground funicular leads up into the lively pedestrianised district of Istiklal Caddesi. The hotel consists of one- and two-bedroom apartments, each with a study, a bathroom and a fully equipped kitchen. They are furnished sensibly yet attractively with warm-coloured period pieces and four-poster beds. From the upper floors there's a good view of the harbour with the skyline of Old Istanbul in the background; you can also enjoy the panoramic restaurant on the top floor. A sauna-Turkish bath and a café hide in the vaulted underground chambers. The pleasantly forthcoming, friendly management is another memorable asset.

rooms	22 apartments: 7 for 2, 15 for 4.
price	Apts for 2, 100 YTL. Apts for 4, 180 YTL.
meals	45-60 YTL, with wine.
closed	Never.
directions	3km from Taksim: off Karaköy Square (difficult car access), two streets below Galata Tower.
airport	15km from Istanbul Airport.

	Cemal Ekingen
tel	+90 (212) 2924841
fax	+90 (212) 2442323
email	info@galataresidence.com
web	www.galataresidence.com

Self-catering

Map 1/City Map p29 Entry 15

Anemon Galata Hotel

Büyük Hendek Cad. 11, Kuledibi, 80020 Istanbul

Istanbul is many cities rolled into one. This one is Galata, once an Italian colony, with a medieval Genoese defence tower rising from its heart. A fashionable district in the 19th century, inhabited by the Europeans and the Jews of the imperial capital, it went down with the empire, then came back 80 years later when the winds of fashion turned once more. The restorers went to work to unearth glimpses of vanished glory – a bit of palatial plaster here, an ebony goddess there, cast-iron railings by the finest Parisian suppliers elsewhere – hidden under layers of slum grime. Anemon Hotel occupies a beautiful old apartment building in Galata Square, right across from the tower. It is operated by the Anemon hotel chain which brings professional expertise to the job, at the expense, perhaps, of a certain amount of personal contact and soul. The lobby glitters impressively; the rooms promise 'old-world' luxury; the view from the glass-enclosed roof café must be among the world's most glorious cityscapes.

rooms	27: 21 twins/doubles, 6 suites.
price	280 YTL. Suites 350 YTL. Singles 230 YTL.
meals	45-60 YTL, with wine.
closed	Never.
directions	2.4km from Taksim: next to Galata Tower.
airport	15km from Istanbul Airport.

Dilvin Aygan
tel	+90 (212) 2932343
fax	+90 (212) 2922340
email	info@anemongalata.com
web	www.anemonhotels.com

Hotel

Taxim Suites

Cumhuriyet Cad. 49, Taksim, 80090 Istanbul

A stylish, sophisticated and comfortable residence just off Taksim Square, the centre of Istanbul's night and business lives. The outer shell is an apartment building from the 1950s; the interior is done in a sleek and modern fashion using quiet natural colours and avoiding all 'Turkisms'. This is contemporary studio design at its cleanest cut: you could just as well be in Kuala Lumpur or Manhattan. The property is managed by Divan Hotels, the oldest – and, in some ways, still the classiest – of Turkish hotel chains. The original Divan Hotel itself is just across the boulevard, which means you can use the hotel's facilities while enjoying the comforts of a private home, pampered by round-the-clock concierge and room service. You have a choice of regular studios and duplex penthouses; a penthouse will, of course, come with a perfectly splendid view over Istanbul's rooftops. All mod cons are supplied, including auto-answer telephone, plug-in internet, DVD player, swish kitchenette and whirlpool bath. They will even take care of your daily shopping list.

rooms	17 apartments: 15 for 2, 2 for 4.
price	Apts for 2, 240 YTL. Apts for 4, 520 YTL. Breakfast extra.
meals	Restaurants nearby.
closed	Never.
directions	In Taksim, opposite Divan Hotel.
airport	20km from Istanbul Airport.

	Merve Çapkan
tel	+90 (212) 2547777
fax	+90 (212) 2562021
email	reservation@taximsuites.com
web	www.taximsuites.com

Self-catering

Villa Blanche

Keskinkalem Sok. 7, Esentepe, 80300 Istanbul

Surrounded by the high-rise office blocks and the chaos and the crowds of one of
Istanbul's principal business centres, Villa Blanche is a pleasant surprise: this quiet
and modest hotel stands in a good-size garden with flowering borders, plenty of
trees and a substantial swimming pool. The furnishings may be rather banal and
repetitive but it makes up in friendly intimacy for what it lacks in fashionable
gloss. Mrs Çerçi is an impressive hostess who runs the establishment with
personal, hands-on style. She appears to be on friendly speaking terms with
everyone who counts in Turkey's business and cultural circles. Her elegant
restaurant serves Turkish and international classics and most of her clients are, of
course, business visitors and company guests. In addition to hotel rooms of
varying size – and one should add, varying states of repair – there are a number of
self-catering apartments, each with its own kitchen and a study; ideal for longer-
term visitors.

rooms	40 twins/doubles + 7 apartments for 4.
price	140 YTL. Singles 100 YTL. Apartments 180 YTL.
meals	30-45 YTL, with wine.
closed	Never.
directions	4km from Taksim: past Şişli, left beside Kuwait-Turk bank on the way to Zincirlikuyu.
airport	20km from Istanbul Airport.

	Ferda Çerçi
tel	+90 (212) 2163719
fax	+90 (212) 2163718
email	villablanche@hotelvillablanche.com
web	www.hotelvillablanche.com

Hotel & Self-catering

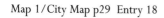

Bebek Hotel

Cevdetpaşa Cad. 34, Bebek, 80810 Istanbul

Here is an insider tip par excellence: a small, clubbish hotel set directly on the seafront in one of Istanbul's most exclusive 'village'-suburbs. With its wonderful position, wizened old waiters and high-living clientele, the bar has been a legend among connoisseurs since time immemorial – and the vista is indeed stunning. The hotel itself, which had been showing its age, was thoroughly renovated a couple of years ago. The new look is a bit posh but still delightfully free of the intrusions of mass tourism. Half the rooms overlook the Bay of Bebek, decidedly the most attractive harbour on the Bosphorus; it's worth paying the extra. To one side stands the old mosque of Bebek, peaceful under its grove of ancient eucalyptus trees. Floating off shore are a few yachts that probably represent a good portion of the national income, and a half dozen of Istanbul's best restaurants are within walking distance (as is McDonald's). The hotel's own Ambassadors Restaurant is an excellent place to savour a fish-and-*meze* dinner in the traditional Bosphorus fashion.

rooms	21 twins/doubles.
price	200–320 YTL.
meals	From 60 YTL, with wine.
closed	Never.
directions	9km from Taksim: on the European shore of the Bosphorus.
airport	24km from Istanbul Airport.

	Oğuz Erdem
tel	+90 (212) 3582000
fax	+90 (212) 2632636
email	bebekhotel@bebekhotel.com.tr
web	www.bebekhotel.com

Hotel

Bosphorus Palace Hotel

Yalıboyu Cad. 64, Beylerbeyi, 34676 Istanbul

The elegant Bosphorus *yalı* of an Ottoman dignitary, the building was restored in the 1990s into an approximation of its original appearance then converted into a hotel of sumptuous opulence. Novelist John Le Carré and international financier Adnan Kashoggi have signed the guest book; Prime Minister Erdoğan chose the top suite for his son's honeymoon. The location is gorgeous indeed: sultans at the neighbouring Beylerbeyi Palace had scarcely a better view of Istanbul's skyline. Impressive, too, are the four-metre-high ceilings, the Regency furniture, the painted mouldings and the tall windows with the waves lapping directly underneath. The style is European rather than Turkish, and the presence of modern hotel fixtures intrudes only lightly on the surrounding sense of richness. Ask for a room with a Bosphorus view. The restaurant, set in the former boathouse, offers an international menu. The hotel is conveniently near the bridge on the Asian bank of the Bosphorus and you can book its private speedboat service from the European side.

rooms	14: 13 twins/doubles, 1 suite.
price	200–420 YTL. Suite 800 YTL.
meals	From 60 YTL, with wine.
closed	Never.
directions	11km from Taksim: near the Asian (eastern) foot of first Bosphorus Bridge.
airport	24km from Istanbul Airport.

İrem Uslu, Özgür Meriçten

tel	+90 (216) 4220003
fax	+90 (216) 4220012
email	info@bosphoruspalace.com
web	www.bosphoruspalace.com

Hotel

Photo Nişanyan Gezi Tanitim Ltd, Selçuk, Turkey

around istanbul

around istanbul: escaping the metropolis

The supply of attractive holiday spots within Saturday motoring distance of Istanbul is surprisingly thin. The northern Marmara coast is hopeless – a vast conglomeration of cheap summer housing and tattered beach motels. The Black Sea coast of Thrace, full of under-used beaches and forested wild hills, remains utterly unexploited.

There is more life in the Asian direction:

- Polonezköy offers the odd whiff of rural Europe on the doorstep of Istanbul
- Ağva is a popular choice, both for its beach and its unexpectedly exotic river
- There are some nice villages in the hills of Yalova, İznik and Sapanca in a refreshingly unspoilt setting of orchards and forest. They offer a bare handful of modest but welcoming farmhouse-hotels set up by urban dreamers in search of their rural idyll
- Slightly further east lies the lovely old town of Mudurnu, which certainly deserves to be known for more than its fried chicken; the Değirmenyeri Houses near Mudurnu are among the happiest discoveries of this book

The beautiful shores of Lake Abant, on the other hand, have little to offer beyond a couple of tired resorts from a past age.

Polka Country Hotel
Cumhuriyet Yolu 36, Polonezköy, 81650 Istanbul

Polonezköy was founded by Polish refugees who were settled in the Sultan's domains after the failed revolution of 1848. With its solid half-timbered farmhouses, small Catholic church and the occasional domestic pig – a shocking sight in a Muslim land (but please read on) – the village feels like a patch of rural central Europe planted at Istanbul's back door. Polka is the only hotel in town that offers some comfort and class while staying true to the spirit of the village. It is housed in a fine old farmhouse that has been renovated in good taste in a contemporary 'mid-European' country fashion. There are plenty of massive timber rafters, comfortable armchairs, log-burning fireplaces, chestnut-wood trimmings and hunting trophies. The restaurant, housed in a converted barn, is among the very few places around Istanbul where you can order pork chops. Weekends can be crowded, especially in spring and autumn, while on weekdays the place has the air of a deserted film set.

rooms	15 twins/doubles.
price	140 YTL. Singles 130 YTL.
meals	45-60 YTL, with wine.
closed	Never.
directions	20km from Istanbul: TEM motorway Kavacık exit, then 14km to Polonezköy.
airport	35km from Istanbul Airport.

	Çiğdem & Murat Dağdelen
tel	+90 (216) 4323220
fax	+90 (216) 4323042
email	polka@superonline.com
web	www.polkahotel.com

Hotel

Map 1 Entry 21

Village Park Country Resort

İshaklı, 81680 Beykoz, Istanbul

Here is a place to keep in mind when you need to flee the big city. Just a 40 minute-drive from the Bosphorus Bridge, it offers fresh meadows, horses and the sweet smell of earth, all hygienically packaged and served by a well-groomed team freshly transferred from one of Istanbul's top chain hotels. In fact, it started out as a dog hotel and obedience-training school. The dogs still occupy one part of the extensive property, but – apart from their propensity to (occasionally) bark in chorus – you need not be aware of their presence. There is space enough to enable you to lose the weekend crowds and to sit by the wooded banks of the river that flows through the grounds. And you are welcome to give a hand with the fledgling organic farm that occupies another part of the territory. The bedrooms are vast and vastly comfortable, furnished in contemporary Scandinavian style. They have fireplaces and whirlpool baths, zillion-channel TVs and plug-in web connections, and panoramic windows that oversee the fields.

rooms	20: 15 twins/doubles, 5 suites for 5.
price	180 YTL. Suites 240 YTL. Singles from 90 YTL.
meals	45-60 YTL, with wine.
closed	Never.
directions	40km from Istanbul: TEM motorway Kavacık exit, 14km to Polonezköy, then 10km toward Şile.
airport	60km from Istanbul Airport.

	İzlem & Serdar Saruhan
tel	+90 (216) 4345999
fax	+90 (216) 4345415
email	villagepark@tnn.net
web	www.villagepark.com.tr

Hotel

Map 1 Entry 22

Piccolo Mondo
Kurfallı, 81740 Şile, Istanbul

Ağva used to be a sleepy fishing harbour that no one ever went to, mostly because of its atrociously twisting road. Then someone discovered the river Göksu meandering lazily two kilometres outside the town. The first riverbank *pansiyon* opened in 1997. Less than a decade on there is now quite a sprinkling of them, each offering the almost identical attractions of waterfront garden, log cabin, winter fires and summer canoeing. Standing a little way up the river bank, Piccolo Mondo is one of the smaller of the bunch and is somewhat quieter than its neighbours. Mr and Mrs Aydın senior bring plenty of professional expertise to the management of their hotel: they gained it when they were innkeepers in Scotland. Now the second generation of the family runs the day-to-day affairs. Though architecturally uninteresting, the main building is most prettily decked out with potted flowers, while the more recent duplex log cabins promise more fun to guests of all ages. A charming and rustic log-and-timber bar hangs out over the river like a ship's deck.

rooms	20 twins/doubles.
price	Half board 160 YTL. Singles 120 YTL.
meals	Half board only.
closed	Never.
directions	31km from Şile: left in Çayırbaşı village; on entering Ağva, right before bridge.
airport	100km from Istanbul Airport.

	Salim & Asuman Aydın
tel	+90 (216) 7217379
fax	+90 (216) 7217380
email	info@piccolomondohotel.com
web	www.piccolomondohotel.com

Hotel

Map 1 Entry 23

Acqua Verde
Kurfallı, 81740 Şile, Istanbul

The Acqua Verde is easily the most popular among the dozen or more hotels lining the riverbank at Ağva. Part of this is due to a famous soap opera that was filmed here in 2004. Weekends can be hell but at other times it is a remarkably green and quiet escape from the tribulations of the big city. The hotel provides an informal boots-and-fireplace setting for a largely young urban clientele. There is a garden-restaurant by the river, a pleasantly 'rustic' lounge and plenty of lawn to spread out on. Bedrooms in the main building are fairly routine but the newer ones in the section at the back show increasing sophistication. You reach the hotel via a curious mechanical raft that is pulled with ropes and pulleys across the river – a slow-moving, green (of course) river that flows through some surprisingly lush parkland. At night, sitting by the camp fire, one is easily transported into a forest camp leagues away from the bustle of the city. And you can pick berries from the bank as you row down to the beach, 800 metres downstream.

rooms	25: 18 twins/doubles, 6 cabins, 1 suite.
price	Half board 200 YTL. Cabins 260 YTL. Suite 300 YTL. Singles from 150 YTL.
meals	Half board only.
closed	Never.
directions	31km from Şile: left in Çayırbaşı village. On entering Ağva, right after bridge; cross river by raft.
airport	100km from Istanbul Airport.

	Gülsun & Hakan Çelen
tel	+90 (216) 7217143
fax	+90 (216) 7218956
email	acquaverde@acquaverde.com.tr
web	www.acquaverde.com.tr

Hotel

Map 1 Entry 24

Authentique Club

Botanik Parkı, Soğanlı, 16580 Bursa

Come to experience a historic Turkish *konak* rebuilt with a flourish on the edge of an attractive park outside Bursa. Several other impressively re-created models of old architecture, recycled as restaurants and shops, surround the cobble-stoned courtyard. Around them lie the municipal gardens. It is a treat to wake up to chirruping birds and to be able to take a bike ride through well-kept woods and lawns so close to the heart of one of Turkey's largest industrial cities. The interior of the hotel makes a half-hearted attempt at keeping up the 'historic' theme: the spirit is closer here to the New Turkey than to the more refined charms of the Old. But the bedrooms are large and furnished with all mod cons. The more expensive suites have marbled Turkish baths and larger-than-king-size beds. The staff are politely efficient and, in summer, the hotel lawn is often used for wedding receptions. A good restaurant and an excellently fitted health spa with heated indoor pool are among the facilities you may indulge in.

rooms	29: 24 twins/doubles, 5 suites.
price	140 YTL. Suites 230 YTL. Singles 100 YTL.
meals	30-45 YTL, with wine.
closed	Never.
directions	2km from Bursa: on Izmir-Istanbul bypass road near Zoo & Botanical Park.

	Orhan Göktaş
tel	+90 (224) 2113280
fax	+90 (224) 2113903
email	info@otantikclubhotel.com
web	www.otantikclubhotel.com

Hotel

Map 1 Entry 25

Safran Hotel

Ortapazar Cad. Arka Sok. 4, Tophane, 16040 Bursa

Bursa used to be a singularly beautiful city before it grew. You get a sense of what it was like when you walk down the very few old streets left around Tophane Square: they are full of gaily-painted houses, quiet little squares and unpretentious old mosques, all miraculously spared the disasters of development. The neighbourhood is right next to the city centre yet conveys a pleasant small-town feel, and the Safran Hotel occupies a restored townhouse in the prettiest of these streets. The saffron-coloured exterior promises much; the interior has been modernised thoroughly – and, one might add, without much sign of imagination. The ground floor restaurant serves good rakı-and-*meze* fare, often accompanied by live *fasıl* music. Bursa retains many memories of the time when it was the first capital of the early Ottoman state. One of its little-known highlights is the garden of dynastic tombs in the cemetery of the Muradiye Mosque; another is the Yeni Kaplıca Baths, the most faultless Ottoman *hamam* in the country.

rooms	10: 9 twins/doubles, 1 suite.
price	100 YTL. Suite 160 YTL. Singles 80 YTL.
meals	30-45 YTL, with wine.
closed	Never.
directions	In Bursa: travel west of centre to Tophane Square.

Mithat Kırayoğlu

tel	+90 (224) 2247216
fax	+90 (224) 2247219
email	safranhotel@yahoo.com

Hotel

Map 1 Entry 26

Mavi Boncuk Guesthouse
Cumalıkızık, 16370 Bursa

Some 200 houses built in traditional Turkish style line the narrow, cobbled streets of Cumalıkızık, a historic village near Bursa that has been declared a national landmark. (Its other claim to fame is that it is the only place in Turkey where they grow raspberries.) Mavi Boncuk Guesthouse is the only accommodation in town – a pair of old village houses which Mr and Mrs Aslan, a retired couple, have adopted with the enthusiasm of newfound love. Their houses have few pretensions of class but they exude a delicious rustic charm with their creaky floorboards, satin coverlets and trousseau-style embroideries. There is a wonderful overgrown garden and a village-style open veranda where one can slouch in comfort the whole day. Güner Hanım serves an excellent breakfast of fresh herbs, good olive oil and homemade bakes. Her homemade noodles (*erişte*) with walnut sauce is nothing short of a masterpiece. Mavi Boncuk signifies Blue Bead, the common Turkish talisman that is meant to ward off the Evil Eye.

rooms	6 twins/doubles/triples.
price	60 YTL. Triples 90 YTL.
meals	20-30 YTL.
closed	Never.
directions	12km from Bursa: İnegöl/Ankara road 9km. Right to Cumalıkızık, up and left in the village.

	Halil & Güner Aslan
tel	+90 (224) 3730955
email	maviboncuk@cumalikizik-maviboncuk.com
web	www.cumalikizik-maviboncuk.com

Guest house

Map 1 Entry 27

İznik Foundation Guesthouse

Sahil Yolu Vakıf Sok. 13, 16860 İznik, Bursa

The tiles of Iznik marked the high point of Ottoman art. The town's famous craftsmen flourished in the 16th century and died when the kilns of Iznik went out of business in the 17th. In the 1990s, a group of highly dedicated amateurs set out to revive the lost art. Their research foundation spawned a workshop which now produces some brilliant answers to questions about the sultans' tile-makers. It is also the focus of various cultural and civic projects that attract a regular string of interesting people from both Turkey and abroad. The guest house of the foundation is officially a separate unit, and it remains mercifully free of any commercial spirit. The comforts may be basic but the company is usually excellent and the pergola-ed garden is a delight in summer. Iznik is in fact ancient Nicaea, better known as the site of the first ecumenical council of Christianity: the guest house is next to the ruins of the palace where the Roman bishops gathered to formulate the Nicene Creed 17 centuries ago.

rooms	9 twins/doubles + 1 house for 6.
price	60 YTL per person.
meals	Meals by arrangement.
closed	Never.
directions	In İznik: main street to lake; 800m left (southwards) down shore; thro' gap in city walls; immed. left.

	Yasemin Koç
tel	+90 (224) 7576025
fax	+90 (224) 7575737
email	info@iznik.com

Guest house & Self-catering

Map 2 Entry 28

Salıcı Evi

Çamoluk, 16860 İznik, Bursa

Your hosts have built a trio of utterly charming log houses in an olive grove overlooking a gasp-inducing view of Lake Iznik. Within hiking distance are several pretty, slumbering villages of ethnic Georgian background, quiet country lanes to stroll along and a wealth of fruit-laden trees that almost invite one to sin. Seven kilometres down the way is the quiet town of Iznik with its friendly market street and attractive waterfront promenade. We couldn't imagine a better place to spend a few days of peace and quiet within three hours' travel of Istanbul. The main house is the real jewel, full of delicious details and inviting corners. It has a large living room with a fireplace, a kitchen, a memorable terrace and two cosy bedrooms that can sleep a total of four to six. The smaller houses are perfect for couples seeking solitude. They were created with evident love and a lot of good taste by this pleasant middle-aged couple who retired to their solitary hillside in order to heal the ravages of a politically active past.

rooms	3 houses: 2 for 2, 1 for 6.
price	100 YTL. House for 6, 350 YTL.
meals	Meals by arrangement.
closed	Never.
directions	12km from İznik: Bilecik road 7km, right through Çiçekli and Çamoluk.

	Zeki & Filiz Salıcı
tel	+90 (532) 3154536
fax	+90 (216) 3402292
email	bilgi@salicievi.com
web	www.salicievi.com

Self-catering

Map 2 Entry 29

Zeliş Farmhouse

Dibektaş Gürcü Mah., Kurtköy, 54600 Sapanca, Sakarya

It is the personality of the owner that makes this such a special place. Zeliş is a former athlete who held several Turkish records in medium-distance running. A woman of extraordinary and infectious energy, she has taken up farm life with the same winning zest as she ran her races. She makes unusual jams and pickles from unheard-of herbs and all sorts of cheeses; she bakes her bread and presses her olives for oil. She also designs her labels, writes her own web site, has built her own oven and rears a menagerie of animals: a veritable whirlwind of productive activity. Above all, she is a gourmet cook of great talent: dinners are feasts of unforgettable variety and generosity. The position is no less impressive. High on a mountain overlooking Lake Sapanca, the farmhouse stands on 300-acres bounded by valley and forest and crossed by a wild mountain stream. The house itself, by contrast, is a rather haphazard affair that was originally built as a weekend home for a family with many guests. Note that some of the rooms share a bathroom.

rooms	8 twins/doubles, some sharing bathroom.
price	Full board 190 YTL. Singles 140 YTL.
meals	Full board only.
closed	Never.
directions	6km from Sapanca Lake: TEM motorway Sapanca exit; west to Kurtköy; up 6km to Dibektaş.
airport	135km from Istanbul Airport.

	Zeliha İrez
tel	+90 (264) 5920585
fax	+90 (212) 2645680
email	zelisciftligi@mynet.com.tr

Guest house

Map 2 Entry 30

Photo Nişanyan Gezi Tanitim Ltd, Selçuk, Turkey

north aegean

north aegean: country chic

The Northern Aegean has been largely spared the torrent of tourism that washes upon its southern shores. The swimming season is shorter and the resorts are mainly geared to the needs of Turkish families on school holidays. Go in the second half of September and you are likely to have the glorious beaches of heavenly azure to yourself.

Increasingly popular with visitors are the half-dozen pretty hill villages that dot the southern slopes of Kazdağı, or Goose Mountain; they gaze from hilltop perches on the over-developed shores of the Gulf of Edremit. The small country hotels of this area are setting the trend for a new Turkish country 'look'.

Assos is another lovely spot, bringing together striking topography, ancient ruins and a primitive village. A series of more or less virgin coves and fishing harbours lie along the steep coast west of Assos.

Turkey's two major Aegean islands, Bozcaada and İmroz, have held on to their characteristic Greekness yet are mercifully free of the overcharged tourist buzz that affects similar islands across the border. A third island, Cunda, hides a small, delightful, semi-deserted town inside its ring of unseemly holiday housing estates.

The Retreat

İbrice Limanı Yolu, Mecidiye, 22800 Keşan, Edirne

The northern shore of the Gulf of Saroz remains a calm backwater. There are no towns to speak of this side of Enez, just a few simple fishermen's shelters – and the abominable housing estates have not made much headway. The sea here is a diver's paradise. The harbour of İbrice consists of two modest *lokantas* for sustenance, a boat shelter and a *jandarma* (police) point, backed by miles and miles of forest. The aptly-named Retreat lies about two kilometres inland, outside the sleepy farming village of Mecidiye. It started out as a diving camp with a friendly restaurant attached to it, then grew by stages into something more substantial when all sorts of people other than divers found it a congenial weekend haven from the city. It has a mixed bag of rooms including a cosy private cottage, a couple of rooms that make a half-hearted attempt at modishness (one with air conditioning), and several houses on stilts whose comforts are minimal. You can walk to the lovely, empty beach (or drive there in five minutes).

rooms	9: 8 twins/doubles, 1 cottage for 2.
price	Half board 130-150 YTL. Singles 65 YTL. Cottage 170 YTL.
meals	Half board only.
closed	Never.
directions	28km from Keşan: Çanakkale road 5km, right to Mecidiye.

Yeşim & Bülent Ertosun

tel	+90 (284) 7834310
fax	+90 (284) 7834386
email	info@siginak.com
web	www.siginak.com

Guest house

Map 1 Entry 31

Barba Yorgo

Tepeköy, 17760 Gökçeada (İmroz), Çanakkale

Turkey's largest Aegean island had a predominantly Greek population until the winds of hatred scattered them far and wide. In contrast to mild Bozcaada further south, it is a mountainous and sparsely populated island. Near its western end is unforgettable Dereköy, a virtual ghost town abandoned by its Greek inhabitants in 1964. Barba Yorgo means Uncle George in Greek. His taverna/inn is tucked away in the small village of Agridia (Tepeköy in Turkish) in the central valley of İmroz. The town has a winter population of 45 but is no ghost: in August it swells to 500 with the returning émigrés. George Zarbozan migrated the other way: after an industrial career in Istanbul he came back to his native village to start a modest taverna, then did up a couple of village houses (some rooms have kitchens), as well as some unfortunate bungalows, to accommodate his guests in all simplicity. The response was overwhelming, though from an unexpected quarter. The taverna fills each night with singers and revellers, almost all city Turks, acting the Zorba to Greek tunes.

rooms	5 + 6: 5 twins/doubles. 2 houses for 6, 4 bungalows for 4.
price	30 YTL per person.
meals	30-45 YTL, with wine.
closed	Mid-September-April.
directions	12km from Kuzu Limanı (ferry port); island ferries (3 a day) from Kabak İskelesi in Gallipoli Memorial Park north-west of Eceabat. Tepeköy is in middle of island.

Yorgo Zarbozan
tel	+90 (286) 8873592
fax	+90 (286) 8873659
email	danisma@barbayorgo.com
web	www.barbayorgo.com

Guest house

Map 1 Entry 32

Rengigül Guesthouse
Atatürk Cad. 31, 17680 Bozcaada, Çanakkale

Rengigül is a perfect little old 'Greek' townhouse full of very personal charm. The owner is a delightful lady who, after spending a lifetime as an educator in Germany, then retired to this cosy half-Greek island where she also owns an art gallery. She cooks marvellously, presents her cooking impressively and is known for her pumpkin soup; her breakfast table – always set communally – is something of a pageant, the most attractive breakfast spread we have come across in the country. Her house is filled with an amazing collection of personal paraphernalia – family pictures, dolls, hats, books, old letters, embroideries, kilims, postcards, porcelain cups, fresh and dried flowers and hundreds of paintings. The rooms (sharing bathrooms) hail straight from grandmother's storybooks. Özcan Hanım rents several self-catering houses in the sleepy old village streets that surround her *pansiyon*, and owns a cottage set among the vineyards inland. It's a mere 10-minute bike ride from the island's best beach and can sleep a group of eight.

rooms	6 + 1: 5 twins/doubles, 1 suite, sharing bathrooms. 1 cottage for 8.
price	80 YTL. Suite 100 YTL. Singles 60 YTL. Cottage 200 YTL.
meals	From 25 YTL, with wine.
closed	February-March.
directions	In Bozcaada: in Old Town near the church.

	Özcan Germiyanoğlu
tel	+90 (286) 6978171
fax	+90 (286) 6978820
email	rengigul2@superonline.com
web	www.rengigul.com

Guest house & Self-catering

Map 1 Entry 33

Kaikias Hotel

Kale Arkası, 17680 Bozcaada, Çanakkale

All things Greek are now very much in fashion among the best-read, best-heeled sliver of Turkish society. So here we have a stylish new hotel built in Greek townhouse style, painted with scenes from Greek mythology, furnished with a collection of antique books on the history of the Orthodox Church and selling museum copies of Trojan jewellery as souvenirs. The music? It's Greek! The people here are stylish, polite and accustomed to serving a highly demanding urban clientele. They also serve good homemade wines. A much-publicised annual event of readings from Homer is held in August under the hotel's auspices; Bozcaada, formerly Tenedos, was where Homer's heroes parked their ships before they went on to hit Troy. The island keeps much of its Greek character, although the Greek inhabitants are now reduced to a tiny minority. The town is charming in a quiet way and an impressive medieval fortress looms above the sea not far from the hotel.

rooms	18: 13 twins/doubles, 5 suites for 4.
price	From 120 YTL. Singles 90 YTL.
meals	Meals by arrangement.
closed	Never.
directions	In Bozcaada: behind the Castle.

	Handan & İsmail Beydili
tel	+90 (286) 6970250
fax	+90 (286) 6978857
email	info@kaikias.com
web	www.kaikias.com

Hotel

Map 1 Entry 34

Akvaryum Pansiyon

Mermerburun Mvk., 17680 Bozcaada, Çanakkale

This friendly little retreat at the deserted southern end of Bozcaada island offers the ultimate in 21st-century luxury: the total absence of electricity. There is no telephone connection either, and no other building within miles – just imagine. A short walk across the heath brings you to one of the prettiest bays of the entire Northern Aegean – a bright blue cove that is called the Aquarium Bay because of its wealth of underwater life. There are a half-dozen other uninhabited coves within walking distance. One can understand why Deniz and Berna came here as diving instructors – and why they could not leave. He is a marine biologist by training, she an Italian philologist and occasional writer. Theirs is a very basic establishment but it is well attended and friendly. A solar heater ensures decent showers, a gas-powered fridge supplies cold beer. And if you are lucky enough to be there at full moon, you may be able to read at night without even a candle.

rooms	6 twins/doubles.
price	80 YTL. Singles 40 YTL.
meals	Meals by arrangement.
closed	December-April.
directions	6km from Bozcaada town: on the south-east corner of the island.

	Deniz & Berna Pak
tel	+90 (286) 6978774
email	denizpak@yahoo.com
web	www.akvaryumbozcaada.com

Guest house

Map 1 Entry 35

MRG Hotel

Ihlamur Sok. 3, 17200 Biga, Çanakkale

Biga is Deep Turkey at its sleepiest — a pleasant middle-class town that seems to offer no reason for the tourist to stop and take heed. Alexander the Great did; and Epicurus, the philosopher of pleasure, invented the idea of hedonism in next door Lampsacus. In addition, Biga makes a convenient overnight stop for the early-morning ferry to Istanbul on the way back from the North Aegean. But the main reason why we would put Biga on the itinerary is this wonderful little hotel that Mr and Mrs Gürkaynak, both university professors, have created with rare charm and sensitivity. The centrepiece of the compound is a historic wooden mansion, delightfully done in the style of the turn of the 20th century. Annexed to it are two modern wings that are hardly less appealing in their set-up. There is an excellent restaurant and a lively pub that comes as a surprise in the sleepy small-town setting. You will probably find the friendly, low-key atmosphere a relief from the pressures of the tourist coast.

rooms	12: 10 twins/doubles, 2 suites.
price	90 YTL. Suites 130 YTL. Singles 65 YTL.
meals	20-30 YTL.
closed	Never.
directions	In Biga: off main square.

	İpek Gürkaynak
tel	+90 (286) 3168800
fax	+90 (286) 3168805

Hotel

Map 1 Entry 36

İmbat Motel

Bademli, 17860 Ayvacık, Çanakkale

Here is a rare unspoiled stretch of the North Aegean shore – a privately owned cove of brilliantly clear and pebbly water backed by a forest of olive trees. The nearest village is miles away and – apart from one holiday conglomerate that reared its ugly head a couple of years ago – you see no blotch on the peaceful Aegean landscape along the dusty five-kilometre drive down to the shore. Imbat is a quiet and relaxing establishment frequented by a remarkably literate set of people. The setting is pretty basic but your hosts – a sharp-witted lawyer and a schoolteacher from the provincial capital – take great pains to maintain a level of decorum that is much appreciated by their guests. One of its most welcome manifestations, for ears accustomed to the din of other mid-budget Turkish beach hotels, is that no music is played on the premises. Three full meals are served each day, each full of old-fashioned Turkish goodies and fresh fish from the boats that ply the gulf: their soothing rat-tat will lull you through the sunrise.

rooms	20 twins/doubles.
price	120 YTL full board.
meals	Full board only.
closed	November–April.
directions	22km from Assos: Gülpınar road 16km. Left after Bademli village, then 5km downhill on poor road.

	Güzin & Seyfettin Yücel
tel	+90 (286) 7370101
fax	+90 (286) 7370102

Hotel

Map 1 Entry 37

Berceste Hotel

Sivrice Feneri Mv, Bektaş, 17860 Ayvacık, Çanakkale

A dream castle built with naïve exuberance, the hotel stands on a wild volcanic hillside about one kilometre above the harbour of Sivrice, perhaps the last undiscovered cove of the North Aegean coast. In the harbour you find half a dozen houses, two fishermen's cafés and a few primitive motels. Beyond are miles of beautiful pebbly shore fringed by olive groves with the mountain rising to great heights behind. Mr Dinçel, a retired officer, receives his guests with friendly hospitality and memorably good cuisine. His rooms are charming, all done in a quirky rustic style featuring four-poster beds and colourful floral prints. There is a solitary beach 400 metres down the lane and the fish reaches your sun-shaded table within hours of leaving the sea. The scene before your eyes is lonely and grandiose, a breathtaking panorama of the sea with the Greek island of Lesbos on the horizon. For seasoned travellers who cherish out-of-the-way experiences, this could well be the highlight of a tour of Turkey.

rooms	9 twins/doubles.
price	120 YTL half board.
meals	Half board only.
closed	November–April.
directions	12km from Assos: Gülpınar road, left in Bektaş village, then 3km downhill.

	Çetin & Dilhun Dinçel
tel	+90 (286) 7234616
fax	+90 (286) 7234617
web	www.assos.de/berceste

Hotel

Map 1 Entry 38

Kaldera

Sivrice Feneri Mvk., Bektaş, 17860 Ayvacık, Çanakkale

Kaldera is on the same wild mountainside as the Berceste, just a little higher up. Here, an Istanbul architect and his wife, a painter with a few years of bohemian Manhattan behind her, have defied wind and snow, goat and peasant, to build their ideal private haven for artists, writers, thinkers and other like-minded guests. The architecture is unabashedly modern – stony grey and angular with lots of wood inside and minimal yet tasteful contemporary furnishings. All rooms have private terraces, suites get kitchenettes. A mini-Stonehenge of basalt pillars adds dramatic effect to the garden, while dabs of colour here, a corner of comfortable cushions there, betray the more feminine hand of Mrs Ersöz. The cuisine, also supervised by Mrs Ersöz in person, is memorably good and nearly all organic, full of fresh local produce and glories of olive oil (cushioned by olive groves on all sides, the Gulf of Edremit claims to produce the best oil in the land). There's a private pebble beach a short drive down the hill and an utterly archaic village, with more goats than people, a few kilometres further up.

rooms	5: 2 twins/doubles, 3 suites for 5.
price	Half board 160 YTL. Suites 200 YTL. Singles 120 YTL.
meals	Half board only.
closed	Never.
directions	12km from Assos: Gülpınar road, left in Bektaş village, then 3km downhill.

	Ahu & Hüsmen Ersöz
tel	+90 (286) 7234420
email	infokaldera@e-kolay.net
web	www.kaldera.org

Old Bridge House

Behramkale (Assos), 17860 Ayvacık, Çanakkale

It is not *grand luxe*. The walled garden is subdivided into a series of imaginative and cosy spaces using recycled material salvaged from junkyards and derelict village houses, there is a grassy lawn for lying around and a campfire for nocturnal guitar-plucking gatherings. In addition to rooms in the happily cluttered main house you have a choice of ramshackle wooden huts in the garden. They stand at the foot of an old stone bridge outside the old village of Behramkale, in glorious view of the acropolis of ancient Assos. Flocks of goats pass each morning led – or followed – by their shepherds. Cem is a born traveller; Diana is Dutch. They met in Laos and lived for a while in Thailand before they decided to make their home in rural Turkey. They cook well when the spirit blows that way, use the internet effectively and could not care less about housekeeping. Latterly, Cem inherited a more conventional hotel down at the harbour of Assos, where he now runs an excellent restaurant. Genuinely laid-back.

rooms	7: 4 twins/doubles, 3 cabins.
price	90 YTL. Singles 70 YTL. Cabins 35 YTL per person.
meals	Meals by arrangement.
closed	Occasionally in winter.
directions	1km from Assos: on Ayvacık road by the old Ottoman bridge.

	Cem & Diana Elmacıoğlu
tel	+90 (286) 7217426
fax	+90 (286) 7217044
email	oldbridgehouse@yahoo.com
web	www.assos.de/obl

Guest house

Map 1 Entry 40

Lembas Houses

Behramkale (Assos), 17860 Ayvacık, Çanakkale

There are plenty of guest houses in the old upper village of Assos but the choices are limited if you are looking for a really special place. Lembas fills a gap in this respect. It offers two independent apartments that are comfortable, aesthetically pleasing and, above all, very private. Yalçın and Övgü gave up big city careers to seek a quieter life with their baby and open their dream café. The studio flat above the café is big, full of light and furnished in a pleasantly simple modern style. It has a large private terrace where you can sunbathe all alone if you wish – although being so close to the café has drawbacks as well as advantages. If you want even more privacy, book into the Stained-Glass House located two blocks away – a pretty old village house in the traditional Assos style with thick stone walls, creaky milk-blue stairs and an enclosed courtyard/garden. It is a short walk up to the acropolis – and a near-vertical two kilometre drive down to the harbour.

rooms	2 apartments for 3.
price	160 YTL. Singles 90 YTL.
meals	Meals by arrangement.
closed	January-February.
directions	In Assos: in upper village.

	Övgü Demir
tel	+90 (286) 7217391
fax	+90 (286) 7217393
email	lembas@superonline.com
web	www.assosonline.com

Self-catering

Map 1 Entry 41

Eris Pansiyon
Behramkale (Assos), 17860 Ayvacık, Çanakkale

Assos flourished in the 4th century BC under the tyrant Hermias, a friend and protector of Aristotle's. The philosopher himself plodded over these grounds when he was banished from Athens for being too friendly with Philip of Macedonia. For Clinton, a poet and novelist of philosophical bent, it was the right place to retire with his wife Emily after teaching in the developing world and finally Istanbul. The American couple took over one of the solid, square old houses of Behramkale, at the foot of the acropolis of Assos, and converted it into a pleasant B&B. They have a bright courtyard filled with flowers and a splendid view over the valley. Inside, the rooms are straightforward with all the essentials and no frills. Emily is a good hostess who does not overlook the little things, such as a welcome cup of tea or an evening cookie (homemade, of course); breakfasts are generous. Eris was, of all things, the goddess of Discord; she gave the proverbial apple to Paris, the good-for-nothing son of Priam, and the Trojan War ensued. (The house came with the name, chosen by a former owner.)

rooms	5: 4 twins/doubles, 1 suite for 4.
price	90 YTL. Suite 100 YTL. Singles from 70 YTL.
meals	Restaurants nearby.
closed	Never.
directions	In Assos: in upper village at the eastern end.

	Emily & Clinton J. Vickers
tel	+90 (286) 7217080
fax	+90 (286) 7217080
email	erispansiyon@hotmail.com
web	www.assos.de/eris

Guest house

Map 1 Entry 42

Assos Guesthouse

Behramkale (Assos), 17860 Ayvacık, Çanakkale

The acropolis of ancient Assos stands on a mighty bluff overlooking the sea from a height of 230 metres; the harbour – half a dozen noisy tavernas and as many hotels – stands on a tiny ledge at the bottom. An archaic and fascinating place, Behramkale huddles behind the acropolis in a warren of old village houses built of red volcanic stone. Most of these houses have been bought up by urban idyll-seekers; a few have been converted into guest houses offering a quieter alternative to the harbour hotels. Assos Konukevi is one of the latter, a friendly and proper house hidden down a picturesque back lane of Behramkale. Your hosts are a retired couple who love to be complimented on the quality of their jams and will be most upset if you step in with dirty shoes. The self-catering cottages each have a cosy living room and two small bedrooms, and surround a sun-filled courtyard with splendid views of both the acropolis and the valley behind.

rooms	3 cottages for 4.
price	100 YTL. Singles from 70 YTL.
meals	Restaurants nearby.
closed	Never.
directions	In Assos: in upper village.

	Cevat & Aytaç Görer
tel	+90 (286) 7217081

Self-catering

Map 1 Entry 43

Troas Motel

Büyükhusun, 17860 Ayvacık, Çanakkale

A modest hotel set in a converted olive press, the low stone building stands in a colourful garden on the edge of the Aegean Sea. In this undeveloped little plain not far from Assos you are surrounded by a few vegetable farms, some olive groves and not much else. The *lokanta* (restaurant) stands under a vine-clambered pergola where pots of red geraniums perch on a garden wall of brown volcanic stone. The sea is pebbly and usually of a striking light-blue colour. At night, the lights of Lesbos flicker in the distance. The rooms are basic: clean, properly plumbed and air-conditioned, with white, crisply dressed beds, they are nevertheless lacking in any real aesthetic sense. Carlos, a former schoolteacher, political activist and a man of immense personal magnetism, is one of the principal reasons for the popularity of the place. Sadly, he speaks little English; but that is no reason to miss the fishing expedition which sails out on most summer afternoons with a majority of Carlos's guests on board.

rooms	17 twins/doubles.
price	Half board 110 YTL. Singles 65 YTL.
meals	Half board only.
closed	Never.
directions	5km from Assos: Küçükkuyu road, right at km 5.

	Halil (Carlos) Ermiş
tel	+90 (286) 7640279
fax	+90 (286) 7640281
email	info@troasmotel.com
web	www.troasmotel.com

Guest house

Map 1 Entry 44

Çetmi Han

Yeşilyurt (Büyük Çetmi), 17980 Küçükkuyu, Çanakkale

A faultless weekend retreat set in a quiet and beautiful village in the foothills of Mount Ida and a mere 15-minute drive from the beautiful Aegean, Çetmi Han is patronised by a polite urban clientele. The village itself was first put on the map 10 years ago by this very establishment. Half a dozen other hotels, some of them posher or more assertive, have opened in the meanwhile. But Çetmi Han remains in most respects the best run and the most welcoming of the lot. The staff has hardly changed in a decade, always a good sign. Your host is a published poet from Istanbul who cut a banking career short for the sake of this country life. He has a wonderful little garden restaurant, lit by candlelight, and plenty of garden terraces for lounging around under the trees. The rooms, fashioned in stone and timber in the rustic style, overlook a gorgeous pine forest with a horizon that is unassaulted by the detritus of modern development – the ultimate treat for western Turkey.

rooms	16: 15 twins/doubles, 1 suite.
price	Half board 160 YTL. Suite 225 YTL. Singles 110 YTL.
meals	Half board only.
closed	Never.
directions	3km from Küçükkuyu: Çanakkale road for 2km, then right.
airport	240km from Izmir Airport.

	R. Fahir İskit
tel	+90 (286) 7526169
fax	+90 (286) 7526488
email	fahir@cetmi.com
web	www.cetmi.com

Hotel

Map 1 Entry 45

Erguvanlı Ev
Yeşilyurt (Büyük Çetmi), 17980 Küçükkuyu, Çanakkale

Yeşilyurt is full of handsome old stone houses and cobblestone lanes while a combination of cypresses, olive trees and umbrella pines gives it something of an Italian air. Forest and mountains engulf the horizon; the sea is near, yet you are leagues away from the beachtown shambles of the coast. The Judas Tree House (that is what Erguvanlı Ev means) hides modestly at the edge of the village facing a quiet valley of pines. It is a pretty building that uses stone, timber and exposed brick to good effect, combining traditional textures with modern details. The owner is a single woman of remarkable and unassertive charm. She retired from a career of social counselling in Switzerland to start this small hotel, where she offers courses on yoga and meditation in addition to more traditional hotel services. Her breakfasts are a delight. The hills abound in lovely hiking trails and the evenings are as peaceful as you could wish them to be.

rooms	8 + 1: 7 twins/doubles. 1 house for 4.
price	Half board 150 YTL. Singles 115 YTL. House 300 YTL.
meals	Half board only.
closed	Never.
directions	3km from Küçükkuyu: Çanakkale road for 2km, then right before Küçükkuyu, in Yeşilyurt village.
airport	240km from Izmir Airport.

	Suna Kurucan Coşar
tel	+90 (286) 7525676
fax	+90 (286) 7525789
email	info@erguvanliev.com
web	www.erguvanliev.com

Guest house & Self-catering

Map 1 Entry 46

Zeytinbağı

Çamlıbel, 10390 Edremit, Balıkesir

Zeytinbağı (the Olive Garden), an altogether delightful little hotel, is run in highly civilised and friendly manner by a trio of urban refugees who clearly enjoy their work. Tuncel Kurtiz is a veteran actor of legendary fame, his brother-in-law, Erhan, is a superbly gifted gourmet cook and Mrs Kurtiz brings a touch of managerial talent into the balance. They have set up in a charming farmhouse that they have rebuilt with some strikingly modern touches and have developed a reputation for producing the best food between Izmir and Istanbul. They also dream of building a grand theatre in the neighbour's garden. It's the sort of place where you might check in for a night on the way through and end up settling for good. The village itself – full of pretty stone houses, donkeys and gnarled locals – is a great relief after the depressing betonvilles of the coast. There are endless forests of olive tree in the background and you actually wake up to the chirping of the birds and the call of the rooster.

rooms	8 twins/doubles.
price	Half board 200 YTL. Singles 150 YTL.
meals	Half board only.
closed	Never.
directions	9km from Edremit: Çanakkale road for 6km, right to Çamlıbel.
airport	215km from Izmir Airport.

	Erhan Şeker, Menend & Tuncel Kurtiz
tel	+90 (266) 3873761
fax	+90 (266) 3873759
email	zeytinbagi@zeytinbagi.com
web	www.zeytinbagi.com

Guest house

Map 1 Entry 47

Annette's House

Zekibey Mah. Neşe Sok. 12, 10400 Ayvalık, Balıkesir

The unpretentious guest house is also Annette Steinhoff's home. A German lady of great charm, she settled in Turkey many years ago. The exterior does not promise much but the interior captivates with its classic Mediterranean elegance – curvy staircase, high ceiling, white-painted wooden trim – and a kitchen that is straight out of an Italian film of the 1950s. The rooms are plain and all bar one are without private facilities, but Annette's excellent cooking and her graceful welcome make up for any shortcomings in comfort. The quiet overgrown garden is a blissful haven on jasmine-scented summer evenings. Old Ayvalık is a labyrinth of narrow lanes and colourfully painted brick houses of thumbnail size. There is a scattering of Greek churches, converted into mosques after the population exchange of 1924, and many ancient factories that fill the air with the sweet smell of olive oil, the town's principal claim to fame.

rooms	8 twins/doubles, only one with own bathroom.
price	45-70 YTL. Singles from 23 YTL.
meals	Meals by arrangement.
closed	Never.
directions	In Ayvalık: "Villager's Market", on west side of old town.
airport	160km from Izmir Airport.

	Annette Steinhoff
tel	+90 (266) 3125971
fax	+90 (266) 3125971
email	annstei@hotmail.com

Guest house

Map 1 Entry 48

Ortunç

Alibey (Cunda) Adası, 10400 Ayvalık, Balıkesir

Compared to its dry and overbuilt harbour, the back of Cunda Island is a surprise: uninhabited and lush, it is full of deserted coves facing a sea speckled with small islands. Ortunç occupies the nicest cove of all. It has a wide grassy garden that edges on the beach and is bounded by trackless forest on all other sides. The sea is always cool and often startlingly clear while the beach brandishes the Blue Flag of the European Environmental Union, given to beaches of outstanding quality. Orhan Tunç, a retired opera singer, rules his territory closely, keeping it on a short leash. His rooms are a row of bungalows, each with a grapevine pergola in front: they offer few frills but they are definitely good enough – charming, even – for a beach vacation. The place is idyllic at either end of the season when it is calm and bright and even the terrace restaurant seems able to cope. It is not always thus in mid-summer when the beach is invaded by day visitors and the leash does occasionally seem to snap.

rooms	22 twins/doubles.
price	120 YTL. Singles 100 YTL.
meals	30-45 YTL, with wine.
closed	October-April.
directions	10km from Ayvalık: on the western coast of Alibey/Cunda Island, 4km from Cunda town.
airport	170km from Izmir Airport.

	Necla & Orhan Tunç
tel	+90 (266) 3271120
fax	+90 (266) 3272082
email	info@ortunchotel.com
web	www.ortunchotel.com

Hotel

Map 1 Entry 49

Aunt Zehra's House

Alibey (Cunda) Adası, 10400 Ayvalık, Balıkesir

Cunda-town is an even purer version of the North Aegean style than Ayvalık; smaller and quieter, full of pretty old houses taking a perpetual siesta under the bright Aegean sun, its waterfront is lined with jolly seafood tavernas. The island feeling is still there, though the island is now connected to the mainland by a causeway. Of all the quaint corners and pretty little old squares, the quaintest is the square – or rather, courtyard – in front of the former church of the Holy Taxiarchs. Auntie Zehra's house stands on this square. Aunt Zehra, whose wit and sparkling blue eyes betray her Cretan roots, is full of brilliant recipes and homespun philosophy. Her son Hasan serves their guests well – when he's up to helping! The house offers basic comfort and little style, although the rooms are meticulously clean and most of them have their own bathrooms. There is a grapevine pergola in front: here you can sit and meditate on the tattered shell of the church opposite or contemplate the world as it passes gently by.

rooms	5 twins/doubles, some sharing bathrooms.
price	90 YTL.
meals	Meals by arrangement.
closed	Never.
directions	8km from Ayvalık: causeway to Alibey/Cunda island; beside main church in Cunda-town.
airport	164km from Izmir Airport.

	Zehra Başbuğ, Hasan Başbuğ
tel	+90 (266) 3272285

Guest house

Map 1 Entry 50

Photo Turkish Culture & Tourism Office

middle aegean

middle aegean:
cradle of civilisation

Greek civilisation first budded in Ionia — the mid-Aegean coast of Asia Minor between Pergamon and Miletus — a hundred years before Athens was ready to follow suit. Thales and Pythagoras debated philosophy in Ionia; the first world map was drawn here, and Ionian cities vied with one other to build the first Greek temple in marble columns.

Today, some of Turkey's most impressive sites of classical antiquity — Ephesus, Pergamon, Didyma, Miletus, Priene and Sardes, as well as Aphrodisias further inland — are to be found here.

Kuşadası, once the touristic hub of the region, has been virtually crippled by developers' greed. İzmir is a good city to live in, but it has little of interest for the casual visitor. Our insider tip is to seek out a couple of small towns that have been sensitively developed over the last ten years:

- Şirince, a delightful old village in the hills only 8km from Ephesus
- Alaçatı, somewhat off the beaten track, but with a fine beach

Both towns have some of the most gorgeous hotels in this book.

Foçantique Hotel

Küçükdeniz Sahil Cad. 154, 35680 Foça, Izmir

Foça is a quietly pleasant Aegean town that enjoys the dual delight of good beaches and few tourists. There is a classic small-town harbour lined with fish restaurants and a proper seafront promenade where families dress up for the evening stroll. Foçantique stands right on the promenade next to a sandy beach where you can still swim safely in the unpolluted harbour. The front is not particularly prepossessing but it conceals a delightful little hotel which the owners converted from an old stone house in 2004. İnci and Alemdar are English-speaking tour guides of the best calibre, full of spark and chatter and easy-going humour. They have furnished their hotel joyfully, with a creative energy that betrays a happy, almost naïve wish to please. Each room is differently decorated; one is blessed with a Turkish *hamam*; some have bare stone walls garnished with rustic plates; others open directly into the walled garden. The open roof café often stays alive until the small hours of the morning.

rooms	11: 10 twins/doubles, 1 apartment for 5.
price	130-150 YTL. Apartment 150 YTL.
meals	Restaurants nearby.
closed	Never.
directions	In Foça: waterfront north of centre.
airport	80km from Izmir Airport.

	İnci & Alemdar Alemdaroğlu
tel	+90 (232) 8124313
fax	+90 (232) 8127616
email	info@focantiquehotel.com
web	www.focantiquehotel.com

Hotel

Map 1 & 4 Entry 51

Taş Ev

175. Sokak 11, 35680 Foça, Izmir

Taş Ev means, simply, the Stone House. The old town of Foça is full of them –
lovely old cottages, now mostly abandoned to their fate and engulfed by the
glories of cheap cement. A Turkish architect resident in Vienna, Mrs
Bretschneider, has done the sensible thing in restoring one of them and turning it
into a modern and comfortable holiday house – the first of its kind in Foça. The
three-bedroom house is furnished with aesthetic sensitivity and equipped with all
mod cons, including a good kitchen. It is absolutely not a hotel but a private
holiday home – perfect for a group of four or six as a base from which to enjoy
this charming and little-sung harbour town. There's a small garden at the back and
a table on the front porch where you can sit all day, in true Mediterranean style,
to watch the neighbours go by. No breakfast is served but the house is quite self-
sufficient if you decide to cook. Otherwise, there are dozens of restaurants lining
the harbour promenade just down the street.

rooms	1 house for 6.
price	110 YTL for two without breakfast.
meals	Restaurants nearby.
closed	15 November-15 April.
directions	In Foça: two blocks in from waterfront.
airport	80km from Izmir Airport.

	Betül Bretschneider, Banu Bozkurt
tel	+90 (232) 8121244
fax	+90 (232) 8121244
email	b.b.bretschneider@utanet.at

Self-catering

Map 1 & 4 Entry 52

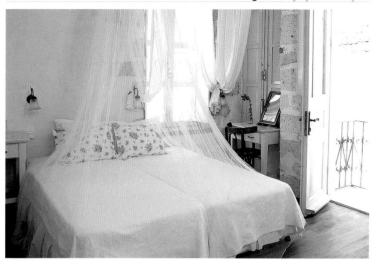

Alaçatı Taş Otel

Kemalpaşa Cad. 132, Alaçatı, 35950 Çeşme, Izmir

A wonderful hotel in a wonderful little town that grew in a few years from sleepy backwater into showcase of rediscovered country chic. Credit for that sweeping transformation goes to Mrs Öziş herself: she set the standards of style with her much-imitated hotel and the houses she designed. It is a natural, simple, unaffected style, unfailing in its command of colour and texture. Like all other buildings in this historic town, Taş Otel (Stone Hotel) is a sturdy old stone house in the neo-classical Greek mould. The blue casements and milky-blue stairway, too, are more reminiscent of that other Aegean coast. Mrs Öziş cut short a high-powered career in marketing to follow a more personal calling in Alaçatı and her bright, girlish manner conceals the businesswoman underneath. She runs the hotel single-handedly and serves superb breakfasts of home-grown jams, olives and village breads under the vines. Full marks for her charming kitchen, her choice of bed linen, her reading cabinet – and the cool swimming pool set in a perfectly peaceful lawn.

rooms	8 twins/doubles.
price	160 YTL. Singles 120 YTL.
meals	Restaurants nearby.
closed	Never.
directions	10km from Çeşme: Çeşme motorway Alaçatı exit, on southern edge of the town.
airport	90km from Izmir Airport.

	Zeynep Öziş
tel	+90 (232) 7167772
fax	+90 (232) 7168517
email	zeynep@tasotel.com
web	www.tasotel.com

Hotel

Map 1 & 4 Entry 53

OEv

Kemalpaşa Cad. 76/A, Alaçatı, 35950 Çeşme, Izmir

Here is a romantic hotel with a deeply feminine touch. The wide arcaded galleries overlooking the inner garden, with low rattan sofas and white curtains fluttering in the wind, look back to the *belle époque* of pre-1922 Smyrna. Mrs Aliberti – who married into one of Izmir's long-established Levantine families – is an elegant hostess. A woman of striking beauty, a former top model and owner of a chic home accessories shop on Izmir's most fashionable street, she fell in love with this old Greek town and decided on a whim to become a hotelier. Her rooms have tall ceilings and high white doors in classic Mediterranean style. The furnishings reflect her own refined taste – and a talent for elegant shopping. Her restaurant aspires to Cordon Bleu status and the pâtisserie serves cakes made by Izmir's most fashionable pastry cook. When Mrs Aliberti has succeeded in acquiring staff to match her own high standards, this will be one of the finest places to stay in the country.

rooms	15: 12 twins/doubles, 3 suites.
price	250 YTL. Suites 300 YTL. Singles from 160 YTL.
meals	45-60 YTL, with wine.
closed	December-15 April.
directions	6km from Çeşme: Çeşme motorway Alaçatı exit; on main street (tricky parking).
airport	90km from Izmir Airport.

	Emel Aliberti
tel	+90 (232) 7166150
fax	+90 (232) 7166152
email	info@o-ev.com
web	www.o-ev.com

Hotel

Map 1 & 4 Entry 54

Sakızlı Han

Kemalpaşa Cad. 114, Alaçatı, 35950 Çeşme, Izmir

Alaçatı used to have an impressive church-turned-mosque, a vegetable market on the main square, a nice café under the mulberry tree – and hundreds of pretty houses that were slowly crumbling under decades of neglect. Times have changed: the high street now flaunts a dozen top-notch restaurants and even more arty boutiques aimed at the ever-growing numbers of tourists, prices boom at the weekend antique market and the over-windy beach has been successfully repackaged as a surfers' mecca. New inns sprout almost monthly in those renovated townhouses. Sakızlı Han (Mastic-Tree Inn) is among the more successful examples of an old house put to new use. The stunning interior seems to leap from the pages of an Italian design magazine; bedrooms are smallish but the technical details are truly superb and the terrace and communal rooms are a delight. The dinner, served in the small walled garden, stands the competition well; a favourable impression remains in the memory of frozen mint lemonade, stuffed squid and mastic-flavoured ice cream.

rooms	8 twins/doubles.
price	180 YTL. Singles 150 YTL.
meals	50 YTL.
closed	Never.
directions	6km from Çeşme: Çeşme motorway Alaçatı exit; on main street (tricky parking).
airport	90km from Izmir Airport.

	Zeynep Şedele
tel	+90 (232) 7166108
fax	+90 (232) 7166109
email	info@sakizlihan.com
web	www.sakizlihan.com

Hotel

Map 1 & 4 Entry 55

Beyaz Han

Kemalpaşa C, Alaçatı, 35950 Çeşme, Izmir

A boutique hotel in neo-Alaçatı style, fashionably designed in a manner calculated to please the newer generation of urban Turks, this classic three-storey townhouse has been rebuilt in concrete and clad in 'natural' stone. A spacious atrium-lobby gives access to stripped-down and fresh-smelling rooms which are positioned somewhat rakishly to line up with the prevailing winds, after which each room is named. Many have high ceilings, canopied beds and ultra-designer washbasins. Communal space consists of an attractively raftered dining room, a sofa in the lobby and a grassy courtyard large enough for two tables; that's it. But then who needs more than a comfortable pillow on which to lay their head when in Alaçatı? The street outside is lively enough with its dozen sophisticated restaurants and all those fashionable boutiques – and it goes without saying that you will spend at least one day at the wind-swept beach two kilometres away, so cleverly reinvented as a surfers' paradise.

rooms	9: 8 twins/doubles, 1 suite.
price	160 YTL. Suite 220 YTL. Singles 130 YTL.
meals	Meals by arrangement.
closed	Never.
directions	6km from Çeşme: Çeşme motorway Alaçatı exit; on main street (tricky parking).
airport	90km from Izmir Airport.

	Fikret Eymür, Turgut Kahraman
tel	+90 (232) 7168453
fax	+90 (232) 7168453
email	info@beyazhan.com
web	www.beyazhan.com

Hotel

Map 1 & 4 Entry 56

Birgicek Hanı

Birgi, 35440 Urla, Izmir

A quiet, pleasant place in a small farming village that lies in the middle of the Çeşme Peninsula, miles from any conceivable tourist destination. Why should one make it out here? We came for the sake of the food and the vineyards, and found it a relief from the depressing holidayvilles of the Çeşme coast. And besides, we like the tang of sheep far more than the smell of suntan oil. The old village inn reportedly dates 'from the Greeks'. It was taken up recently by a pair of very charming urban ladies who had no background in running a hotel – even less in repairing an unwieldy old inn – but loved to cook and wanted to live in the country. They still treat customers as personal guests. The rooms are furnished with old armchairs and grandma's wedding quilts with a faint touch of the attic about them. It is just half an hour from Izmir and there are some lovely walks in the hills – as long as you avoid the furnace-hot months of July and August.

rooms	4 twins/doubles + 1 cottage for 6.
price	60 YTL. Singles 30 YTL. Cottage 80 YTL.
meals	30-45 YTL, with wine.
closed	Occasionally in winter.
directions	45km from Izmir: Çeşme motorway Zeytinler exit, then 2km to Birgi.
airport	60km from Izmir Airport.

	Ayla Tunç, Ayşe Halimoğlu
tel	+90 (232) 7626437
fax	+90 (232) 7626405

Guest house & Self-catering

Map 1 & 4 Entry 57

Han Otel

Camii Atik Mah. Tatar Cami S, 35430 Urla, Izmir

Urla is actually two towns – a coastal town of tedious summer blocks and an old town, hidden away a few kilometres inland, that appears to have been caught in a time warp sometime around the mid-1940s. It has a lively little marketplace of pergola-ed bazaar streets and tiny sun-filled squares where old people still speak the dialect of Crete and shops carry hand-painted signs. The market inn of Old Urla must have been here, unchanged, since at least the 1880s, if not the 1780s. It underwent a thorough restyling a few years ago – not a stylish restyling, really, but we find it naïve and utterly charming in a homely and honest way. There is a proper walled yard for your horse and cart in case you bring one along and a comfortable living room where Mrs Girgin serves delicious homemade food in the company of some cats and the blaring television. The rooms are spartan but clean and airy.

rooms	10 twins/doubles.
price	75 YTL. Singles 50 YTL.
meals	20-30 YTL.
closed	Never.
directions	35km from Izmir: in Urla town centre.
airport	42km from Izmir Airport.

	Ünzüle Girgin
tel	+90 (232) 7542077
fax	+90 (232) 7541092
email	beychany@hotmail.com

Guest house

Map 1 & 4 Entry 58

Yorgo Seferis Evi

Yalı Cad. 47, 35430 Urla, Izmir

The Nobel laureate Greek poet George (Yorgo) Seferis lived in this small town near Izmir before the storms of the early 20th century tossed his community to the opposite shores of the Aegean Sea. His childhood home decayed into a derelict warehouse. Then Greece and Turkey became bosom friends again and Mr Sümer, a photographer, had the brilliant idea of reviving the Seferis house as a cultural landmark and a guest house. He has done an excellent job of rekindling the historic atmosphere, creating a series of thoroughly cosy interiors and furnishing them with antiques of the sort the poet would have felt quite at home with in his childhood. Mrs Sümer makes a friendly hostess. Overall, this is a homely and comfortable hotel with plenty of good sense and not a whiff of high-cultural pretension. The neighbourhood has some good (if expensive) seafood restaurants and several beaches favoured by weekenders from Izmir.

rooms	14 twins/doubles.
price	90 YTL. Singles 60 YTL.
meals	20-30 YTL.
closed	Never.
directions	In Urla Harbour, one street back from waterfront. 30km from Izmir.
airport	42km from Izmir Airport.

	Muzaffer & Şermin Sümer
tel	+90 (232) 7520414
fax	+90 (232) 7523514
email	info@yorgoseferis.com
web	www.yorgoseferis.com

Hotel

Map 1 & 4 Entry 59

Antik Han

Anafartalar Cad. 600, Mezarlıkbaşı, 35240 Izmir

Here is a hotel with character in a city that is sometimes a bit short on that quality. Once, a long time ago, the Antik was one of Izmir's leading inns. Then it suffered the inevitable decline, was somehow spared the inevitable demolition, and was eventually inherited by two young partners who bravely set out to reverse the clock. They have done a good job of creating a friendly, comfortable and unassuming city hotel with a modern interior and all the usual conveniences. The shady inner courtyard makes a friendly oasis in the humid heat of an Izmir summer. Anafartalar Street is one of Izmir's hidden jewels – an old-fashioned shopping street full of colour and commotion, with ivy-twined pergolas and chatty shopkeepers and old tailor shops still ticking away on 1930s Singer sewing machines. Round the corner you find the Agora of ancient Smyrna, a vast and nearly derelict field of Roman ruins that has yet to see the tourist crowds.

rooms	30 twins/doubles.
price	80 YTL. Singles 60 YTL.
meals	20-30 YTL.
closed	Never.
directions	In Izmir: near ancient Agora.
airport	15km from Izmir Airport.

	Cem & Selim Egeli, Türkân Altı
tel	+90 (232) 4892750
fax	+90 (232) 4835925
email	info@otelantikhan.com
web	www.otelantikhan.com

Hotel

Map 1 & 4 Entry 60

Naz Han

St Jean Cad. 1044 Sok. 2, 35920 Selçuk, Izmir

Here is a small guest house that stands out among the swarm of modest, family-run guest houses dotting Selçuk's old quarter below the Castle. The hosts left their city careers behind to pursue a dream in the more relaxed climate of the south. Theirs is a civilised little retreat from the raucous world of tourist Ephesus. A leafy courtyard cluttered with bric-a-brac and artworks collected over a lifetime leads to the charming living room. The guest rooms are fairly basic but have character, and the ones on the upper floor are to be preferred: they are bigger and have more light; it may be worth paying a little more for a room with air conditioning. From the roof terrace you can look out across the whole town – it is a fine spot in which to enjoy Mr Erdoğan's inspired cooking. Up the street lies the ruined Basilica of St John, a massive early-Byzantine edifice in which the evangelist is believed to be buried. The celebrated museum of Selçuk is a couple of blocks down and the ruins of Ephesus lie half an hour away on foot.

rooms	5 twins/doubles.
price	55-65 YTL. Singles from 35 YTL.
meals	Meals by arrangement.
closed	Occasionally in winter.
directions	In Selçuk: near St John's Church.
airport	58km from Izmir Airport.

	Nazan & Kemal Erdoğan
tel	+90 (232) 8928731
fax	+90 (232) 8920011
email	nazhan@superonline.com
web	www.etkinlikturkiye.com/nazhan

Guest house

Map 1 & 4 Entry 61

Nilya

Atatürk Mah. 1051 Sok. 7, 35920 Selçuk, Izmir

Nilya is a comfortable small hotel hidden behind high courtyard walls in Selçuk's old quarter. Mrs Kaytancı runs her indoor republic with friendly elegance. She and her husband, formerly a senior civil servant, left the big city a few years ago to settle in this sleepy Aegean town. She serves superb breakfasts and treats her guests with the sort of easy kindness that is considered perfectly natural in this country but never ceases to amaze visitors from stiffer lands. The bedrooms, surrounding a peaceful arcaded court, are rather small but comfortably and charmingly furnished. The communal rooms, by way of contrast, are decorated with an extraordinary wealth of personal objects and artworks that promise hours of close investigation if you enjoy such discoveries. Below the hill lies the grand sweep of the plain of Ephesus where several millenia of history lie just below the surface – also rich in atmosphere but not so easy to examine at close quarters.

rooms	11: 10 twins/doubles, 1 suite.
price	80 YTL. Suite 120 YTL. Singles 50 YTL.
meals	Meals by arrangement.
closed	Occasionally in winter.
directions	In Selçuk: near St John's Church.
airport	58km from Izmir Airport.

	Nilgün Kaytancı
tel	+90 (232) 8929081
fax	+90 (232) 8929080
email	nilya_ephesus@hotmail.com
web	www.nilya.com

Guest house

Map 1 & 4 Entry 62

Nişanyan House Hotel
Şirince, 35920 Selçuk, Izmir

An elegant small hotel in the historic village of Şirince, owned and managed by the authors of this guide who apologise forthwith for so blatantly promoting their own stuff. We offer two types of accommodation. The Inn has five guestrooms, a library, plenty of lounges and a small restaurant. Furniture includes antiques left by favourite aunts. From the terrace there's a great view over the village rooftops and across unspoilt hills. Then there are several houses clustered along the old cobble-stoned village lanes. One hundred and fifty years old on average, they were renovated using the traditional methods and converted into comfortable houses of considerable charm. Each sleeps two to five people well. One has its own Turkish bath; another has a huge platform bed in the old Aegean fashion. Ephesus is just 11km away, the beach is a little bit farther, and nearly everything worth seeing in the Aegean region is within day-trip distance. Yet the village itself is so enchanting you may wish they weren't.

rooms	5 twins/doubles + 3 houses for 4-6.
price	130-150 YTL. Singles from 85 YTL. Houses 200 YTL for two.
meals	45-60 YTL, with wine.
closed	Never.
directions	8km from Selçuk: turn at northern end of Selçuk to Şirince, right on unpaved road at village entrance.
airport	64km from Izmir Airport.

	Müjde & Sevan Nişanyan
tel	+90 (232) 8983208
fax	+90 (232) 8983209
email	hotel@nisanyan.com
web	www.nisanyan.com

Hotel & Self-catering

Map 1 & 4 Entry 63

Kilisealtı Pansiyon

Şirince, 35920 Selçuk, Izmir

A modest, friendly guest house in the prettiest of Turkey's Aegean villages. There are potted geraniums by the gate and fresh flowers in the vases. The rooms are bright and fresh-smelling, sweet with kilims and grandmother's embroideries. The garden, shaded by a pergola of grapevine, faces a postcard-perfect view of the historic village. The neighbour's elderly donkey provides the wake-up service. Young Fatoş and her little son go out of their way to make their guests feel at home; having worked for years at perfecting the breakfast service at Nişanyan House (see entry 63), she concocts a superb breakfast, served under the tangerine tree. There are about 10 other *pansiyons* in Şirince but none that we had so far felt comfortable about recommending as a good low-budget alternative to our own place further up the hill. The little guest house under the old church – that is what Kilise Altı means – at last seems to fill that particular gap.

rooms	5 twins/doubles.
price	80 YTL. Singles 55 YTL.
meals	Meals by arrangement.
closed	Never.
directions	8km from Selçuk: turn at northern end of Selçuk to Şirince, below the church at village entrance.
airport	64km from Izmir Airport.

	Fatoş Sengül
tel	+90 (232) 8983128
fax	+90 (232) 8983209
email	info@kilisealti.com
web	www.kilisealti.com

Guest house

Map 1 & 4 Entry 64

Villa Konak

Yıldırım Cad. 55, 09400 Kuşadası, Aydın

It is a surprise to find this attractive garden – with no outward clue whatever to its existence – in the middle of Kuşadası's urban labyrinth. It is actually three or four old gardens seamed together: one is shaded by a magnificent magnolia, one has the swimming pool and a century-old well sits in the third. Everywhere there are ancient marble fragments and the sweet scent of citrus trees permeates the air. Contributing to the atmosphere of peace and quiet is that fact that no children under 12 are allowed on the premises. The hotel has become the passion and hobby of its owner, Mr Enderin, since his retirement from a career in finance. He shares his talent for cooking with his wife and will be glad to display it if given proper advance warning. Bedrooms are spotless and have all you need, staff are lovely, tranquillity reigns. Yet a short walk down the hill Kuşadası beckons with the round-the-clock glitter of its tourist bazaars. It used to be a pretty town before it mutilated itself in a fit of building frenzy in the 80s and 90s.

rooms	22 twins/doubles.
price	80 YTL. Singles 50 YTL.
meals	Meals by arrangement.
closed	November–April.
directions	In Kuşadası Old Town: up from municipal baths (Belediye Hamamı).
airport	90km from Izmir Airport.

	Kaya & Türkan Enderin
tel	+90 (256) 6122170
fax	+90 (256) 6131524
email	info@villakonakhotel.com
web	www.villakonakhotel.com

Hotel

Map 1 & 4 Entry 65

Medusa House
09270 Didim, Muğla

Right next to the Temple of Apollo at Didyma, the greatest of the surviving monuments of Greek antiquity in Turkey, the sturdy old stone house stands in the affectionate embrace of its effusive Mediterranean garden, full of bright colours and scents and sweet seating corners. At night, once the tour buses have left, you can slip secretly into the temple grounds and revel in the glory of the 2,000-year old marble. Mustafa is a dynamic local entrepreneur, always full of enthusiasm and projects. Ingrid is an educational officer and politician in her native Germany. They share their life between the two countries and provide a happy mixture of 'Turkish' warmth and 'German' sense of detail to a literate circle of guests from around the world. The inn doubles up as the headquarters of a local Greek-Turkish friendship initiative and the rooms are fairly basic but not without charm. The beach of Didim, sadly over-developed, lies four kilometres away. Far more interesting are the swamplands of the Küçükmenderes delta where vast flocks of water fowl, including the pink flamingo, gather in winter.

rooms	9: 7 twins/doubles, 2 apartments.
price	90 YTL. Apartments 125 YTL. Singles from 60 YTL.
meals	20-30 YTL.
closed	November-February.
directions	In Didim: next to the Apollo Temple.
airport	41km from Bodrum Airport.

	Mustafa Şentürk
tel	+90 (256) 8110063
fax	+90 (256) 8110267
email	medusahouse@aol.com
web	www.medusahouse.com

Guest house

Map 4 Entry 66

Club Natura Oliva

Kocaorman Mah., Pınarcık, 48200 Milas, Muğla

The hotel consists of a series of simply-built cottages set in an almost boundless olive grove dominating the mysterious and beautiful panorama of Lake Bafa. The grounds, sun-drenched and filled with Mediterranean scents, feel more like a farmstead than a hotel garden. Hens roam freely, working away to supply the breakfast table; the olive oil is delicious; the rooms are basic, though each has the civilised comfort of a working fireplace and a private terrace. It is not a place where one would expect to be pampered and spoilt, but it can be a magical spot for the self-reliant. Mrs Koch, hardworking and chain-smoking, runs the show in laconic style, and groups of environmentally-minded Germans arrive from time to time under the auspices of the Munich-based Club Natura. Perfect quiet reigns at other times. There is a sandy beach by the lake and an islet offshore with the ruins of a fortified 12th-century monastery. The strangely shaped volcanic slopes of Mount Latmos conceal more monasteries, some prehistoric paintings and many hermits' cells, accessible only on foot.

rooms	34 twins/doubles.
price	85 YTL. Singles 45 YTL.
meals	20-30 YTL.
closed	Never.
directions	38km from Milas: Söke road, on lakeshore.
airport	55km from Bodrum Airport.

	Aysel Koch
tel	+90 (252) 5191072
fax	+90 (252) 5191015
email	info@clubnatura.com
web	www.clubnatura.com

Hotel

Map 4 Entry 67

Agora Pansiyon
Kapıkırı, 48200 Milas, Muğla

An enchanting place on the roadless north shore of Lake Bafa, wher the old village of Kapıkırı blends with the ruins of Heracleia-by-Latmos. An extinct volcano rises in the back, hiding the ruins of a dozen mediaeval monasteries in its folds. An islet bearing another Byzantine monastery faces the village beach; it was here that Selene, the moon goddess, fell in love with the shepherd Endymion as he lay asleep by the shore, asked Zeus to grant the youth perpetual sleep and bore 50 children from their nightly encounters. Agora is the last primitive among a handful of rudimentary *pansiyons* that exist in the village. It consists of a few modest bungalows in a flower-filled garden to which several more comfortable 'modern' rooms were added a couple of years ago. Mr Serçin, formerly the village *muhtar*, runs the house with his wife and daughters, still full of eager and erratic hospitality after all these years. There is good fresh seafish from the fisheries of Dalyan, and hiking tours can be organised into the fantastic boulderlands of Beşparmak Mountain upon request.

rooms	14: 11 twins/doubles, 3 cabins, some sharing showers.
price	Half board 100 YTL. Singles 80 YTL.
meals	Half board only.
closed	Never.
directions	39km from Milas: Söke road, right (northwards) at Çamiçi, 11km to Kapıkırı.
airport	52km from Bodrum Airport.

	Orhan Serçin
tel	+90 (252) 5435445
fax	+90 (252) 5435567
email	info@herakleia.com
web	www.herakleia.com

Guest house

Map 4 Entry 68

Dülgeroğlu Hotel
Cumhuriyet Meydanı 1, 64100 Uşak

An unexpected treat in deep, provincial Turkey. The building was a commercial warehouse built in 1898 by some Frenchmen in the style of Hausmann's Paris – a sort of Galeries Lafayette lost in dusty Anatolia. After rotting gently for a century, it was acquired by a local industrialist who renovated it for the sake of putting some life into this somnolent town. The result is quite brilliant: there is a lofty atrium café that would look at home in Paris – give or take a potted palm tree or two – a perfectly done bar/pub and comfortably styled and polished rooms. The staff display that remarkably genuine – if slightly bumbling – hospitality that disappeared long ago from the more touristy parts of the country but still forms the chief joy of travelling in deepest Turkey. The reason a tourist would go to Uşak is this: to seek out the Treasure of Croesus, a spectacular collection of Lydian funeral finery from the 6th century BC. This was once held by the Metropolitan Museum of New York but reverted to its town of origin after a famous legal battle.

rooms	20: 15 twins/doubles, 5 suites.
price	90 YTL. Suites 105 YTL. Singles 70 YTL.
meals	20-30 YTL.
closed	Never.
directions	In Uşak: near Museum.

	Mehmet, Necdet Dülgeroğlu
tel	+90 (276) 2273773
fax	+90 (276) 2273606
email	info@dulgeroglu.com.tr
web	www.dulgeroglu.com.tr

Hotel

Map 1 & 4 Entry 69

Photo Nişanyan Gezi Tanitim Ltd, Selçuk, Turkey

south aegean

coastal playground 1

A spectacularly indented coast, a rugged and green interior and a string of sleepy harbours basking in the shadow of medieval castles makes this south-western corner of Turkey irresistible. A cloudless sun warms the turquoise waters by day; by night, the deafening song of the cicadas drowns the distant rumble of a thousand discotheques.

Bodrum Peninsula, particularly the trendy north, attracts a cosmopolitan Turkish crowd, while the beach resorts of the south still draw much of their custom from the north of England. Marmaris is a modern city that serves the yachting fraternity well, while the jagged double-peninsula to its west hides a dozen little-known and unspoiled villages against a striking natural backdrop.

Two smaller towns deserve mention on the way further south: Dalyan, as sleepy as its rumbling river, and Göcek, a haven for yachtsmen. In Fethiye, the centre of the tourist activity has shifted to the beach of Ölüdeniz, 12km away, and the various coastal villages. Even the once inaccessible coast of Faralya now has a paved road.

4reasons hotel + bistro

Bakan Cad. 2, Yalıkavak, 48930 Bodrum, Muğla

The four reasons that the owners imply in their name are Serenity, Design,
Quality and Attitude. The fifth – Intellect – comes as a welcome bonus. From this
hilltop spot you will spend time stretching your eyes over a pretty view of
evergreen citrus gardens and the island-studded sea beyond. The pool lies utterly
serene in a grove of olives. Your hosts, who abandoned successful North American
careers in marketing communications early to enjoy a more civilised life here,
have a bright, unstuffy approach to things; their sense of design is elegantly
modern without losing either its soul or its touch of humour. The rooms seek
harmony in simplicity: some beds repose on a floor of smooth white pebbles that
soothe the feet first thing in the morning. The restaurant justifies a visit in its own
right. Modestly dubbed a 'bistro', it promises the easy comforts of an American
diner but yields a cuisine of skill and finesse. A vegetable garden on the premises
supports an emphasis on crisp textures and fresh tastes.

rooms	18 + 1: 13 twins/doubles, 5 family suites. 1 apartment for 6.
price	261-342 YTL. Family suites from 410 YTL. Singles from 211 YTL. Apartment 522 YTL.
meals	45-60 YTL, with wine.
closed	7th January-March.
directions	19km from Bodrum: turn right in Yalıkavak toward Tilkicik.
airport	48km from Bodrum Airport.

	Esra & Ali Akın
tel	+90 (252) 3853212
fax	+90 (252) 3853229
email	info@4reasonshotel.com
web	www.4reasonshotel.com

Hotel & Self-catering

Map 4 Entry 70

Lavanta Hotel

Papatya Sok. 32, Yalıkavak, 48400 Bodrum, Muğla

The view is marvellous, the breakfast excellent, the rooms luxurious. But what brings so many correspondents to write to us so effusively about Lavanta Hotel appears to be something more: it is the sense of being the personal guests of an urbane, courteous and witty landlord. Tosun Merey is a businessman who spent most of his life in various countries around the world. He and his German-born wife planned Lavanta first as a private home. They then took it on with the enthusiasm of second youth, and ended up transforming a hundred acres of virgin hillside into a comfortable and spacious retreat. They offer their guests excellent cuisine and all the attention to detail that turns a good hotel into an extraordinary one. Each room is differently furnished, each stands a notch or two above the usual 'five-star' standard. Apartments are cheerfully and stylishly decorated; bathrobes and pool towels are provided. There is a good library – and several sitting rooms filled with valuable Asian antiques.

rooms	8 + 12: 8 twins/doubles. 6 apartments for 2, 6 apartments for 4.
price	From 230 YTL. Singles 180 YTL. Apartments for 2, 250 YTL. Apartments for 4, 480 YTL.
meals	45-60 YTL, with wine.
closed	November-March.
directions	15km from Bodrum: turn left 1km before Yalıkavak.
airport	48km from Bodrum Airport.

	Maria & Tosun Merey
tel	+90 (252) 3852167
fax	+90 (252) 3852290
email	lavantahotel@compuserve.de
web	www.lavanta.com

Hotel

Map 4 Entry 71

Adahan

Çökertme Mvk., Yalıkavak, 48400 Bodrum, Muğla

The imposing portals of a *kervansaray* lead into a cloistered courtyard that is centred on a quasi-Roman swimming pool and sprinkled with judiciously chosen antiques. Paintings carry the signatures of nearly every major Turkish artist and the music is classical. Yet fear not: this is by no means swank city, it's a friendly place run by jolly and courteous people. Mr Özyağmur is known to the Turkish public as the author of a weekly column on pet care – and has been at different times a student activist, a photographer, an antique dealer and a professional cabinet-maker. His wife, the steadying element of the duo, has happily recovered from a freak medical condition that had darkened their lives for several years. Together they offer first-rate neo-Mediterranean cuisine, keep a good wine cellar and mount occasional art exhibitions in their hotel. The sea is a five-minute walk away and a colourful weekly market is held on Thursdays just outside. (The ubiquitous Ada was Queen of Halicarnassus and a friend of Alexander the Great. You can see her reconstituted body in the castle of Bodrum.)

rooms	24: 18 twins/doubles, 6 suites.
price	120 YTL. Suites 160-200 YTL. Singles from 100 YTL.
meals	30-45 YTL, with wine.
closed	November-March.
directions	15km from Bodrum: turn left in Yalıkavak centre, behind marina.
airport	48km from Bodrum Airport.

Mine & Cihan Özyağmur
tel   +90 (252) 3854759
fax   +90 (252) 3853576
email info@adahanotel.com
web   www.adahanotel.com

Hotel

Map 4 Entry 72

Karakaya Meditation Center

Karakaya M, Gümüşlük, 48400 Bodrum, Muğla

The sort of 'development' that turned Bodrum into the proverbial playground has so far missed the hamlet of Karakaya, snuggled under its black rock (kara kaya) in a hidden valley above Gümüşlük. A few goats and a dozen upper-class Turks in search of elusive peace are all that live there. Cactus and geranium grow wild in the courtyards. There is erratic electricity but no streets of any sort. To reach some houses, you climb rock-to-rock like a goat. The builders have been closing in and the idyll may not last much longer, but it is a beautiful place while it lasts, a genuine 'primitive' that lovers of Mediterranean sights and textures will adore. It is also the perfect place for a meditation camp that aims to bring people into a closer awareness of their selves. The camp offers a spirit of community and very basic accommodation – bungalows, tents and a dorm – drawing a highly international crowd with European as well as South Asian participants. Weekly programmes cover spiritual healing and pulsation, sufism and shamanic energy, though there is no obligation to join. The food is vegetarian.

rooms	6 bungalows and tents for 2 or 4, sharing showers.
price	From 20 YTL per person; half-board encouraged.
meals	Low-cost meals.
closed	November-April.
directions	20km from Bodrum: right before Gümüşlük, 3km to Karakaya village.
airport	50km from Bodrum Airport.

	Alp Ekşioğlu
tel	+90 (537) 4339361
email	kun@oshokun.com

Camp

Map 4 Entry 73

Ada Hotel

Tepecik Cad. 128, Türkbükü, 48400 Bodrum, Muğla

This place is a gem of contemporary Mediterranean style, full of delicious textures and fascinating details: despite the sophisticated hints of Turkish style, it would be at home on one of the posher hillsides of the Côte d'Azur. A highlight is the Turkish bath, possibly the most elegant to have been built in Turkey in the last century. We also love the private suite with its tatami-mat flooring, royal four-poster and a whirlpool bath set among stone slabs under a skylight. There are little private terraces filled with sunlight, a gnarled olive tree framed by plate glass and some serious antique carpets on the floors; two suites share a pool, and there's a shuttle to the beach. A good collection of French wines lurks somewhere behind the crypt, which serves as the winter restaurant. Türkbükü itself, clustered irregularly around its crescent-shaped waterfront, is trying hard to become the Turkish Saint Tropez; your hotel is tucked away on the hill surrounded by the summer compounds of Bodrum's newly rich, a 10-minute walk up from the waterfront where a stunning beach café and fully-crewed yacht await your orders.

rooms	13: 7 twins/doubles, 3 suites for 2, 1 suite for 3, 2 family suites.
price	430 YTL-470 YTL. Suites up to 780 YTL.
meals	From 60 YTL with wine.
closed	November-March.
directions	20km from Bodrum: uphill in Türkbükü.
airport	45km from Bodrum Airport.

	Vedat Semiz, Ayşe Nur Gedik
tel	+90 (252) 3775915
fax	+90 (252) 3775379
email	info@adahotel.com
web	www.adahotel.com

Hotel

Map 4 Entry 74

Maki Hotel

Keleşharımı Mvk. Mimoza Sok., Türkbükü, 48400 Bodrum, Muğla

Türkbükü is the trendiest spot on the Bodrum Peninsula. A prodigious number of designer-casual restaurants line the crescent-shaped harbour; sunbathing platforms take up much of the rest. On a summer's day it is sometimes hard to walk along the waterfront without stepping on some famous body. Having added 20-plus rooms this year, smothering the hills with steel and concrete, Maki is no longer a small hotel. Why do we love it? Perhaps because we went to visit in October not July. The crowds gone, Türkbükü is still beautiful: at sunset, with great cypresses casting their shade on the swimming pool and a string of islets lying temptingly quiet on the horizon, it is hard to resist its allure. The hotel is impeccably, expensively styled and its cuisine is probably the best in a town that thrives on the reputation of its eateries. The location is perfect: at the more desirable far end of the corso and a pebble's throw from the sea... cushioned decking for sunbathing lines the water's edge. The swishest beach bars, peopled by prowling paparazzis and boozed-out celebrities, lie within strolling distance.

rooms	37: 20 twins/doubles, 17 suites.
price	340 YTL. Suites 450–900 YTL.
meals	From 60 YTL, with wine.
closed	Never.
directions	23km from Bodrum: on Türkbükü waterfront.
airport	53km from Bodrum Airport.

	İrfan Kuriş, Alper Yüceer
tel	+90 (252) 3776105
fax	+90 (252) 3776056
email	info@makihotel.com
web	www.makihotel.com

Hotel

Map 4 Entry 75

Queen Ada Hotel

Hoşgörü Sok. 7, Torba, 48400 Bodrum, Muğla

A small stylish hotel that combines an idyllic position with good cuisine and a serene sundeck over its own little beach, the Queen Ada aims to provide all the frills (maids and laundry), thrills (water skiing) and gadgets of a chain hotel on an intimate scale. The surroundings are beautiful: a meticulously landscaped garden hugs the lovely pebbled beach and the pool is a wonderfully calm pond wedged between sea and countryside. Beyond it lie the ruins of a massive Byzantine monastery and the undeveloped hills. All rooms open directly onto the garden, the majority with a sea view. They are a good size, furnished very correctly in modern style, and strive bravely to offer everything that a modern traveller is expected to need. Extras include a pillow menu (six choices, all synthetic) and a well-gadgeted fitness room. More memorable is the cuisine, in which Mr Ülkümen, a former engineer now in personal charge of his hotel, takes a close interest. The menu brings together inspired touches from around the globe and excellent wines accompany a variety of unusual cheeses.

rooms	22: 21 twins/doubles, 1 suite.
price	350-450 YTL. Suite 670 YTL.
meals	From 60 YTL, with wine.
closed	November-March.
directions	7km from Bodrum: at the eastern end of Torba Bay.
airport	30km from Bodrum Airport.

	Umut Ülkümen
tel	+90 (252) 3671598
fax	+90 (252) 3671614
email	queenad@attglobal.net
web	www.queenadahotel.com.tr

Hotel

Map 4 Entry 76

Su Hotel & Cottages

Turgutreis Cad. 1201 S, 48400 Bodrum, Muğla

A friendly medium-budget hotel, partly English-owned, that offers two separate types of accommodation. The hotel proper lies hidden in a traffic-free back lane of Bodrum, a big swimming pool forming the centrepiece of an intimate courtyard smothered in flowering bougainvilleas. The buildings, which multiplied suddendly in 2005, are styled in vivid colours and filled with the whimsical charm of patchwork quilts, stencilled vine branches and comfortable old armchairs. It is secluded and quiet, yet within walking distance of the main centres of the town's lively nightlife. Two streets from the hotel, the newer annexe consists of two attractive stone cottages in Bodrum's archaic, blocky style. The cottages are furnished in good taste in a Mediterranean-Nordic mix, and provide plenty of living space for a couple or a family with children. The walls incorporate blocks of stone from the Mausoleum of Halicarnassus, one of the Seven Wonders of the ancient world, whose modest foundations lie a couple of streets away.

rooms	12 + 2: 10 twins/doubles, 2 suites. 2 cottages for 4.
price	140 YTL. Suites 160 YTL. Singles 80 YTL. Cottages 270 YTL.
meals	30-45 YTL, with wine.
closed	Never.
directions	In Bodrum: off Turgutreis Street (one-way traffic eastwards), difficult car access.
airport	38km from Bodrum Airport.

	Zafer Küstü
tel	+90 (252) 3166906
fax	+90 (252) 3167391
email	suotel@superonline.com
web	www.suhotel.net

Hotel & Self-catering

Map 4 / City Map p30 Entry 77

Antique Theatre Hotel

Kıbrıs Şehitleri Cad. 243, 48400 Bodrum, Muğla

A stylish and luxurious small hotel that stands out for its stunning view over Bodrum's magnificent double harbour. The architecture reflects the cascading white steps of the ancient theatre of Halicarnassus which lies across the busy highway behind. The garden, designed by a dean of Turkish architects, manages to squeeze a large number of cosy, private spaces into the limited premises. The rooms are decorated with a serene elegance using bone-coloured hand-woven fabrics, fine candles and old prints of naval scenes; some have great ocean views. The pool is a marvel: lying at the edge of a terrace with no railing between it and the void, it seems to float weightlessly above the spectacle of the bay. A majority of the guests are Americans: they appear to savour the pampering service of the French-accented gourmet restaurant which once was the subject of a flattering review in the *New York Times*. Breakfast is a banquet of breads and cheeses, olives and walnuts, fruits and cherry jams. The owners, an art historian and a banking executive, are occasionally present.

rooms	18: 17 twins/doubles, 1 suite for 4.
price	210-270 YTL. Suite 670 YTL.
meals	From 60 YTL, with wine.
closed	Never.
directions	In Bodrum: on bypass road opposite the antique theatre.
airport	38km from Bodrum Airport.

	Selmin & Zafer Başak
tel	+90 (252) 3166053
fax	+90 (252) 3160825
email	theatrehot@superonline.com
web	www.antiquetheatrehotel.com

Hotel

Map 4/City Map p30 Entry 78

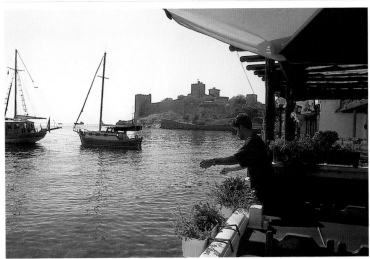

Baç Pansiyon

Cumhuriyet Cad. 14, 48400 Bodrum, Muğla

You couldn't get any closer to the heart of Bodrum than this. The famous Main Alley is right on your doorstep, thronged hip-to-tanned-hip until five in the morning. The sea is in behind, the waves spraying first-floor windows on windy days (we saw someone casting a fishing line from the breakfast table – really!). The stupendous Castle of the Crusaders, floodlit at night, almost bursts into your bedroom. A hundred restaurants, and as many fashionable bars, lure the hungry, the thirsty, the needy who pass within strolling range. Baç Pension shines amongst the half-dozen rather tired hotel-pensions in this area with its excellently designed – almost opulent – interior. The staff are friendly, almost to a fault. Rooms are big, some with marvellous enormous windows over the sea; the rest face the street. And if you tend to worry about street noise… why in the world would you be in Bodrum if you plan to go to sleep before sunrise?

rooms	10: 8 twins/doubles, 2 suites.
price	90-105 YTL. Suites 115 YTL. Singles 70 YTL.
meals	Restaurants nearby.
closed	Never.
directions	In Bodrum: east of the Castle, difficult car access.
airport	38km from Bodrum Airport.

	Sedat Baç
tel	+90 (252) 3161602
fax	+90 (252) 3167917
email	bacpansiyon@turk.net

Guest house

Map 4/City Map p30 Entry 79

Merve Park Suites Hotel

Atatürk Cad. 73, 48400 Bodrum, Muğla

A well-designed, small 'urban' hotel in downtown Bodrum that uses its limited space with great efficiency. The decoration is quintessential neo-Bodrum – all terracotta and wrought iron, Greek mouldings and earthenware pots. An outstanding collection of antiques furnishes the lobby and the other communal areas and guests can actually make a bid to buy the furniture – or dip into the owner's own extensive collections. A highly-regarded art gallery is also attached to the hotel. On the upper level, the lovely swimming pool and leafy inner garden give you a snap-perfect view of the harbour. Easy car access is another plus, given the cramped Bodrum streets and traffic nightmare. And it's in a great position, near the far end of the town's legendary harbour promenade – a mile-long alley of innumerable twists and turns, lined with street cafés and stuffed with well-tended bodies on summer nights. The most popular (and the noisiest) nightlife venues are clustered up this end.

rooms	19: 17 twins/doubles, 2 suites.
price	130 YTL. Suites 150 YTL. Singles 80 YTL.
meals	Restaurants nearby.
closed	Never.
directions	In Bodrum: eastern end of town.
airport	38km from Bodrum Airport.

	Ömer Musa Önat
tel	+90 (252) 3161546
fax	+90 (252) 3161278
email	mervepark@yahoo.com

Hotel

Golden Key Bodrum

Kumbahçe Mah. Şalvarağa Sok. 18, 48400 Bodrum, Muğla

At the heart of Turkey's favourite summer playground, this deluxe small hotel has all the attractions and trappings of a well-equipped, almost luxurious, summer villa. Like thousands of similar villas splattered across the hills of Bodrum, the building affects a modern approximation of the town's traditional all-white cubic architecture. It stands on the seashore in a new part of town that is conveniently close to the old harbour promenade. The small artificial beach in front is good for a morning swim but, better still, you can use the hotel's own excursion boat to explore the glorious coves around the next cape. From the terrace you have a view of the harbour of Bodrum dominated by its medieval castle – particularly fabulous at night. The establishment consists of eight comfortable suites and a separate self-catering residence consisting of two bedrooms and a living room that's big enough for social occasions. This served in the past as a pied-à-terre for former Prime Minister Mesut Yılmaz.

rooms	8 suites + 1 apartment for 6.
price	280 YTL. Apartment 560 YTL.
meals	45-60 YTL, with wine.
closed	November-April.
directions	In Bodrum: eastern end of town.
airport	39km from Bodrum Airport.

	Gülören Polikar
tel	+90 (252) 3130304
fax	+90 (252) 3134171
email	bordum@goldenkeyhotels.com
web	www.goldenkeyhotels.com

Hotel & Self-catering

Map 4/City Map p30 Entry 81

Atami Hotel

Cennet Koyu, Gölköy, 48400 Bodrum, Muğla

In a lovely spot by a private cove surrounded by forest, yet only 20 minutes from Bodrum and even less from the jazzy harbour of Türkbükü, the Atami Hotel stands right by the sea. The narrow pebbly beach has wooden swimming platforms that allow you to dive directly into the deep clear waters. The only other buildings in sight are the modest shacks of a fishery on the opposite side of the bay. Some excursion boats prowl the bay during the day but perfect quiet reigns at night. Your hosts are a Turkish-Japanese couple who live here with their delightful daughter Ebru: their hospitality is full of charm and modesty, qualities sometimes in short supply on Bodrum's well-heeled peninsula, and the meticulous grooming of the gardens certainly shows a Japanese hand. The building itself is an architectural disaster but the rooms at any rate are comfortably and pleasantly furnished, and have balconies with lovely views. There is even a grand piano on the premises.

rooms	32 twins/doubles.
price	210-320 YTL. Singles 160 YTL.
meals	45-60 YTL, with wine.
closed	Never.
directions	23km from Bodrum: unpaved road east of Gölköy.
airport	42km from Bodrum Airport.

	Atakan & Midori Öztaylan
tel	+90 (252) 3577416
fax	+90 (252) 3577421
email	info@atamihotel.com
web	www.atamihotel.com

Hotel

Map 4 Entry 82

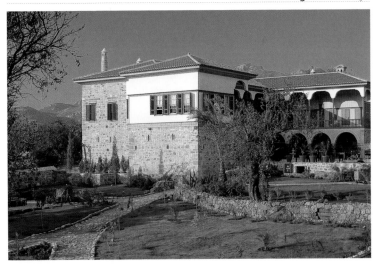

Mehmet Ali Ağa Konağı

Reşadiye, 48910 Datça, Muğla

The main room, a dazzling firework of colour and detail, must be one of the world's 10 most spectacular hotel rooms. The building itself is a work of art. Its maker was the Lord of Datça in the early 19th century, when the writ of the Ottoman state hardly reached these parts. The re-maker is a businessman of private means who has poured a fortune into the challenge. It is a work of obsessive passion, and a world-class restoration. The original house is revived in precise fidelity, down to 70,000 individually hand-forged nails and untold cubic metres of sweet-smelling cedar wood. An army of specialist painters restored the wall paintings, and the original *hamam* has been revived. The result exudes elegant repose — a very 'oriental' sort of aristocratic poise, less cluttered and less noisy than its European counterparts of the same era. The modern wing, which holds most of the bedrooms, shows much refinement in its own right. Ms Pir, daughter of the owner, runs the hotel with understated grace and friendly courtesy.

rooms	17: 15 twins/doubles, 1 suite for 2, 1 suite for 4.
price	290-470 YTL. Royal suite 510 YTL. Singles 230 YTL.
meals	45-60 YTL, with wine.
closed	Never.
directions	4km from Datça: Marmaris road 4km, left in Reşadiye.
airport	158km from Dalaman Airport.

	Sena Pir
tel	+90 (252) 7129257
fax	+90 (252) 7129256
email	senapir@kocaev.com
web	www.kocaev.com

Hotel

Map 4 Entry 83

Gabaklar Pansiyon

Kızılbük Mvk., Mesudiye, 48920 Datça, Muğla

At Hayıtbükü there are half a dozen ramshackle *lokanta-pansiyons*, ten farmhouses and a few moored boats by the waterfront. And if that is too much for you, then try Kızılbük, another bay half a mile to the east. It has two farmhouses, some tangerine groves and only one *lokanta* with rooms. At the Pumpkins' (for that's what the family name means), there are few amenities and little pretension to style, but the atmosphere is warm, the garden pretty and the fish ever fresh and delicious. The newly-built bungalow-cottages for two may be aesthetically disastrous but they leave little to be desired in terms of basic uncomplicated comfort. The beach is 50 metres away and belongs to you alone. The sea is as beautiful as the Mediterranean can be. A surprisingly high-calibre clientele from the big city enjoys here the sense of being very far away from the nonsense of modern-day civilisation.

rooms	26: 12 twins/doubles, 14 cabins.
price	100 YTL. Cabins 120 YTL. Singles 60 YTL.
meals	20-30 YTL.
closed	Never.
directions	21km from Datça: Knidos road 11km; left to Mesudiye; down to coast at Hayıt Bükü; left and continue 1km to next bay.
airport	180km from Dalaman Airport.

	Mustafa & Server Avcı
tel	+90 (252) 7280158
fax	+90 (252) 7280171
email	gabaklar@hotmail.com
web	www.gabaklar.com

Guest house

Map 4 Entry 84

Dede Pansiyon
Eski Datça, 48900 Datça, Muğla

Set three kilometres inland from the port, Old Datça is a delightful village of honey-coloured stone houses in gardens of pomegranate and fig. No blemish disturbs the eye along the main street as it winds between garden walls overflowing with bougainvillea and jasmine. Dede Pension, in the middle of these sensualities, is one of the finest examples of the rustic style we have came across in Turkey: it manages to be neat and in good taste without succumbing to the lure of designer chic. The attractive stone buildings stand in a large and sunny garden full of fruit trees, hidden nooks, stairways and back doors. The swimming pool is beautiful, even luxurious. A 1952 Prestcold refrigerator stands at the poolside bar looking as elegant as a pink swan. Rooms are furnished with charm and white linen; each has its own kitchenette. They are named after artists (Dalí, Chagall, Chaplin. . .) reflecting the İpeks' long involvement in the art and theatre circles of their adopted home city of Berlin.

rooms	6 apartments for 2.
price	100 YTL.
meals	Restaurants nearby.
closed	Never.
directions	2km from Datça: Marmaris road 2km, left to Eski Datça/Dadia.
airport	160km from Dalaman Airport.

	Hacer & Gültekin İpek
tel	+90 (252) 7123951
fax	+90 (252) 7123951
email	dedepansiyon@superonline.com
web	www.dedepansiyon.com

Guest house & Self-catering

Map 4 Entry 85

Villa Carla

İskele Mah. (PK 50), 48900 Datça, Muğla

Villa Carla stands atop a high cliff outside Datça, commanding a broad sweep of the Mediterranean with the Greek islands of Symi and Rhodes on the horizon. A steep footpath leads down to a secluded cove where you will find a pebbly private beach and good snorkelling. As little as a decade ago, this was total wilderness; now urban Datça threatens to close in with its unseemly holiday compounds. Villa Carla is a quiet, friendly and comfortable hotel which easily conveys a sense of home. The new management under Mr Sancaktar, an architect, has breathed new life into the place after a couple years of wobbly uncertainty. The breakfast is once again excellent, the staff is eager and quick, and even the old tradition of five o'clock tea and pastries has been revived to happy effect. Beyond Datça, the peninsula remains one of the wildest and most spectacular corners of the Turkish Riviera, with endless possibilities of exploration by boat and on foot, especially in the cooler days of spring and autumn.

rooms	18 twins/doubles/triples.
price	90 YTL. Singles 50 YTL.
meals	20-30 YTL.
closed	Never.
directions	2km from Datça: Kargı road past the southern end of town.
airport	168km from Dalaman Airport.

	Bülent Sancaktar
tel	+90 (252) 7122029
fax	+90 (252) 7122890
email	info@villacarladatca.com
web	www.villacarladatca.com

Hotel

Map 4 Entry 86

Château Triopia

(PK 39), Yaka, 48920 Datça, Muğla

It is the site rather than the actual building – a mini-château built by an old Istanbul boy who spent most of his life as a bank official in Austria – that conjures up visions of grandeur. The Datça Peninsula gets wilder and more spectacular as you go west towards the desolate tip of Cnidus. The valleys are filled with vast groves of almond which bloom a in a magnificent pink flood in February. A 400-metre pyramid of rock, crowned with remnants of the temple of Apollo Triopion, stands opposite the hotel. The buildings combine a sturdy mid-European country look with the familiar lines of Turkish summer-house architecture; you get balconies with views of the sea, small kitchens, big bathrooms and colourful, if timid, touches of Hundertwasser and Gaudí. Mr Orel is especially proud of his cuisine, which combines a fusion of European and Asian influences with a wide-ranging wine list. The hotel owns a private bay near the ruins of Cnidus, 10km away: the old three-room cottage there could be a lovely place to spend a night in total solitude.

rooms	10 apartments for 2-4.
price	90 YTL. Singles 70 YTL.
meals	30-45 YTL, with wine.
closed	Never.
directions	17km from Datça: on Knidos road, west of Yaka village.
airport	178km from Dalaman Airport.

	Alper Orel
tel	+90 (252) 7255522
fax	+90 (252) 7255170
email	triopia@msn.com
web	www.triopia.net

Hotel & Self-catering

Map 4 Entry 87

Golden Key Hisarönü

Hisarönü, 48700 Marmaris, Muğla

This calm beach resort with a beautiful garden, managed with professional élan, faces the splendour of the Gulf of Hisarönü, framed by rank upon rank of jagged mountains marching into the blue haze. The villa-type sleeping quarters surround a swimming pool buried in a riot of flowering and perfumed Mediterranean bushes. A spreading lawn borders the private beach of red sand while a brisk westerly wind disperses the afternoon heat. Six villas are divided into comfortable two- and four-bed suites. A luxury villa sleeping up to 10 is sometimes available, too. The décor, which uses exposed timber and quilted patchwork textiles, manages to convey a warm, personal feel. Mrs Uyar makes an utterly charming host and she presides over a young and eager team, dividing her time between Hisarönü and Golden Key's other property at Bördübet, 20km away. Hisarönü itself is no more than a cluster of beach hotels and villas. The hills are full of wild forest paths and unspoiled harbour villages lie within an hour's drive through some of the most spectacular scenery of the Aegean coast.

rooms	18: 12 suites for 2, 6 suites for 4.
price	Half board 270-450 YTL. Singles from 200 YTL.
meals	Half board only.
closed	November-April.
directions	24km from Marmaris: Datça road for 17km; left to Hisarönü from Bozburun junction.
airport	115km from Dalaman Airport.

	Şebnem Uyar
tel	+90 (252) 4666384
fax	+90 (252) 4666042
email	hisaronu@goldenkeyhotels.com
web	www.goldenkeyhotels.com

Hotel

Map 4 Entry 88

Golden Key Bördübet

Bördübet, 48700 Marmaris, Muğla

The forest site, far from most signs of human intrusion, is magical. The giant pines and lush undergrowth are fed by a stream that runs through the hotel grounds and is filled to the brim with fat fish and tortoises. An army of geese raises a racket at one end of the generous property but the air is everywhere heavy with the scent of wild honey and forest soil. The surveyors who named the site in the past were astonished by the variety of bird-life and Bördübet is said to be a corruption of the apparently English word 'birdbed'. The hotel is a number of two-storey buildings that blend unobtrusively into the quasi-tropical landscape. Rooms come in three different categories and, although none is quite royal except in name, they are tastefully outfitted in modern country-style furniture especially designed for the hotel. You can either take a boat or walk 20 minutes down the forest road to reach the beach, a totally private cove provided with those civilised necessities that are a good restaurant, a long wine list and a set of good CDs.

rooms	22 suites.
price	Half board 300-380 YTL. Singles 230 YTL.
meals	Half board only.
closed	November-April.
directions	31km from Marmaris: Datça road for 14km; right in Değirmenbaşı (poor road).
airport	130km from Dalaman Airport.

	Şebnem Uyar
tel	+90 (252) 4369230
fax	+90 (252) 4369089
email	bordubet@goldenkeyhotels.com
web	www.goldenkeyhotels.com

Hotel

Map 4 Entry 89

Amazon Club

(PK 45), Bördübet, 48700 Marmaris, Muğla

In deep, wild forest far removed from all jarring traces of modern development, is a remarkable camping site. The founder and ruler of Camp Amazon is Mr Güneş Tecelli, a retired journalist of legendary fame. His wit and sense of humour are evident in many small details around the camp. In addition to plenty of space to pitch your tent, the grounds have a nice swimming pool, a vine-shaded restaurant of local repute and a number of basic but spotless cabins (made of pumice stone) scattered under the pine trees, with private showers and loos. A quiet stream trickles through miles of lush wilderness in the background. No alligators – although you'd almost expect to find them here – but rabbits and hens for the children. You can walk from the camp to a deep and deserted bay that rejoices in spectacularly clear water and a small private beach where you are unlikely to see more than a dozen bathers at any time. In addition to the semi-paved road from Değirmenyanı, there is a more scenic gravel road that branches off from the narrowest point of the Datça Peninsula and skirts the sea.

rooms	16: 14 cabins for 2, 2 cabins for 4.
price	Half board 100 YTL. Cabins for 4, 200 YTL.
meals	Half board only.
closed	November-April.
directions	27km from Marmaris: Datça road 14 km; right in Değirmenbaşı; right again at the end of the road (poor road).
airport	135km from Dalaman Airport.

	Kaan, Özge, Cengiz Tecelli
tel	+90 (252) 4369111
fax	+90 (252) 4369160
email	amazon@klupamazon.com
web	www.klupamazon.com

Camp

Map 4 Entry 90

Sabrina's House

Bozburun, 48700 Marmaris, Muğla

The best thing about this Mediterranean idyll is that it is not accessible by car: you are either picked up by boat from a pier or you walk 15 minutes from the end of the road through gardens and open country. The other good thing is Tobias, your wonderfully relaxed and relaxing host who is likely to arrive at the pier on his homemade raft fitted out with a grand sofa, a glass of iced whisky at the ready. Squeezed between bare rocks and the sea on the far shore of Bozburun's convoluted gulf, Sabrina's is an enchanting garden bursting with flowering plants. The rooms have evolved patchwork-wise over the years, with plenty of charm and good sense. Some are basic; others leave nothing to be desired, including an outdoor whirlpool bath and fantastic harbour view. Swimmers may use the small private beach on the edge of the garden or borrow one of several boats of various descriptions which stand around waiting for guests to embark. There is a scattering of deserted islands featuring mysterious ruins within 30 minutes' rowing distance.

rooms	13 twins/doubles.
price	140-210 YTL. Singles 100 YTL.
meals	20-30 YTL.
closed	15 November-March.
directions	3km from Bozburun: Söğüt road; right to Hotel Mete; call for boat or walk 15 mins from end of road.
airport	132km from Dalaman Airport.

	Tobias Knörle
tel	+90 (252) 4562456
fax	+90 (252) 4562470
email	sabrinashaus@superonline.com

Hotel

Map 4 Entry 91

Villa Julia

Kızılyer Mah., Söğüt, 48700 Marmaris, Muğla

Penny and David are the owners of Rhea, a grand old centenarian topsail schooner that they charter for weekly cruises. They fell in love with this sleepy little faraway cove many years ago and built their modest Mediterranean hideaway right on the edge of the sea. It is a house with a homely and 'English' feel to it, a sandy beach at its doorstep and a porch that induces laziness; you can dive from the private jetty or slip into the pool. The owners are often away at sea; in their absence, a young woman from the village runs the house with a big smile and lots of practical sense for what appears to be an almost exclusively English clientele. Within strolling distance is Söğüt, one of the last remaining primitive villages on the Turkish Mediterranean coast, and its pair of utterly unpretentious seaside *lokantas*. It has no shorefront 'boulevard' yet, so fishing boats can be moored right next to people's front doors. Jagged mountains surround the bay and the Greek island of Simi rises like a wall on the horizon.

rooms	6 twins/doubles.
price	120 YTL. Singles 80 YTL.
meals	Meals by arrangement.
closed	November-March.
directions	6km from Bozburun: right to Söğüt, first right to Kızılyer harbor, right along the beach.
airport	140km from Dalaman Airport.

	David & Penny Ross
tel	+90 (252) 4965001
fax	+90 (252) 4965001
email	sailandvilla@aol.com
web	www.sailingandvillaholidays.com

Guest house

Map 4 Entry 92

Palmetto Hotel

Selimiye, 48700 Marmaris, Muğla

Selimiye is a lazy waterfront village. Nothing happens most of the time: the cicadas sing, a fisherman sitting in his boat may occasionally rev his engine or the old folks sitting in the café may shift a chair. In spring, the orange blossoms smell overwhelmingly sweet. The harbour is nearly landlocked, enclosed by mighty mountains, and has an islet in its centre with a ruined fortress on it. The town was practically inaccessible by car until 20 years ago. Now there are a few restaurants catering to the visiting yachts and a few decent places to stay, of which Palmetto is easily the most comfortable. The host here is a charming medical professor whose past includes a career in the United States. The staff go out of their way to please. There is a spotless and curvaceous pool and a nice grassy sward where you can lie down for a tan. The sea is somewhat shallow but it is, after all, right on the doorstep. So never mind the architecture: *boşver* – 'never mind' – is, as a boat in the harbour proclaims, the motto in Selimiye.

rooms	18 twins/doubles.
price	160 YTL. Singles 135 YTL.
meals	30-45 YTL, with wine.
closed	Never.
directions	38km from Marmaris; to Selimiye via İçmeler-Bayır or Hisarönü-Orhaniye (twisting road in both cases).
airport	120km from Dalaman Airport.

	Erol Üçer, Zafer Pekçedenöz
tel	+90 (252) 4464299
fax	+90 (252) 4464301
email	palmettoresorthotel@hotmail.com
web	www.palmettoresort.com

Hotel

Map 4 Entry 93

Club Çobantur

Akyaka, 48700 Marmaris, Muğla

The setting is delightful – a small peaceful cove off the west end of Akyaka town, surrounded by forest and occupied by a few low-key buildings (though more are sprouting each year). An almost completely virgin stretch of the Aegean coast starts here and continues nearly 100 spectacular kilometres west to Bodrum. For most of the way it is served only by a bumpy gravel road and the sea is of an unreal indigo colour. You may be able to talk the hotel staff or the neighbouring fishermen into lending you a rowing boat to explore the shores in total quiet. The hotel itself is a modern and relatively unimaginative building with largeish rooms and all the usual comforts. It has a nice big garden with a duck pond and a proper quay equipped to handle yachts. The restaurant serves staple *mezes* and a range of grills, often to the accompaniment of live popular music. Mr Özer and his team succeed in making most guests happy with their eager, urgent hospitality.

rooms	27 twins/doubles.
price	120-180 YTL. Singles from 63 YTL.
meals	30-45 YTL, with wine.
closed	Never.
directions	30km from Marmaris: follow eucalyptus drive to Akyaka; 2km west of town.
airport	68km from Dalaman Airport.

	Mesut Özer
tel	+90 (252) 2434550
fax	+90 (252) 2434558
email	clubcobantur@cobantur.com
web	www.club.cobantur.com

Hotel

Map 4 Entry 94

Pupa Yat Hotel
Adaağzı, 48700 Marmaris, Muğla

A small hotel in a quiet and beautiful setting by the sea, far removed from Marmaris's decibel belt, the Pupa Yat lies in a well-established garden of palm trees and shady eucalyptuses on the edge of the region's famed liquidambar forests. There is a small private beach and a yacht anchorage with a distant panoramic view of the harbour of Marmaris. The hotel and the adjoining facilities are run by a yacht charter agency as a base for their sailing clients. Non-sailors, however, are equally welcome – and not always outnumbered. The building, a plain functional block from the 70s, has recently undergone some renovation. It has modestly furnished and bright rooms, each with a balcony and a sea view, while the sea breeze makes the restaurant a delightful spot for an evening drink. Marmaris combines a spectacularly beautiful setting with a ruthless pace of growth that has managed to wipe out every trace of charm and tradition in less than 30 years. A taxi stand at the hotel gate makes it easy to get about.

rooms	19 twins/doubles.
price	90 YTL. Singles 65 YTL.
meals	45-60 YTL, with wine.
closed	Never.
directions	5km from Marmaris: Aksaz road 4km, right toward Adaköy.
airport	90km from Dalaman Airport.

	Alex Örme
tel	+90 (252) 4133566
fax	+90 (252) 4138487
email	hotel@pupa.com.tr
web	www.pupa.com.tr

Hotel

Map 4 Entry 95

Villa Florya
Kumlubük, 48700 Marmaris, Muğla

Kumlubük, meaning 'sandy cove', lies within sight of the harbour of Marmaris but is cut off from it by a forbidding set of limestone mountains. Development here is still embryonic and the two-mile-long beach of black sand remains uncrowded except for the midday rush of tour boats. Behind the beach, a handful of farmhouses and a few shabby hotels stick out of the citrus gardens; the ruins of ancient Amos lie undisturbed in the scrub at the top of the cliff. Villa Florya stands dramatically on a great mass of rock that juts into the sea in the middle of the beach: a large, unwieldy garden rises in rocky tiers to the three-storey block perched on the summit. The rooms in the main building are unexciting but their view is out of this world; some more elegant suites were added on the flat ground below in 2005 and the new management under Mr Dörtçelik seems well-relaxed. But, above all, swimming off the deserted beach in the early morning one feels that neither time nor the petty details of service must count for too much in paradise.

rooms	16: 12 twins/doubles, 4 suites.
price	120 YTL. Suites 160 YTL. Singles from 100 YTL.
meals	30-45 YTL, with wine.
closed	November–March.
directions	16km from Marmaris: south via İçmeler and Turunç to Kumlubük, half way along the beach.
airport	100km from Dalaman Airport.

	Nevzat Açıkgöz, Levent Dörtçelik
tel	+90 (252) 4767553
fax	+90 (252) 4767554
email	info@villaflorya.com
web	www.villaflorya.com

Hotel

Map 4 Entry 96

Happy Caretta Hotel

Maraş Cad. Ada S, 48840 Dalyan, Muğla

A happy, unpretentious little hotel set directly by Dalyan's river in full view of the Lycian royal tombs, Caretta is easily the best among some 20 family-run *pansiyons* and modest hotels lining this bend in the river. The very welcoming hosts – İlknur, Münir, their small daughter, three dogs and two rabbits – run a peaceful, homely establishment. The garden lies in the shade of century-old cypresses: it is an ideal place for lazy days lulled by the hypnotic monotone of the river boats. The rooms, on the other hand, have little to write home about; the loft feels more like a vast and cluttered family room than a hotel lounge. The distance to the town centre is just right: far enough from the evening crowds yet a mere five minutes by bicycle. It is possible to swim in the river if you don't mind the occasional inquisitive turtle; otherwise it is a half-hour river boat ride through the vast water-logged labyrinth of the delta to one of Turkey's best beaches.

rooms	14 twins/doubles.
price	70 YTL-100 YTL. Singles from 50 YTL.
meals	Meals by arrangement.
closed	Occasionally in winter.
directions	In Dalyan: left at centre, downriver.
airport	28km from Dalaman Airport.

	İlknur & Münir İdrisoğlu
tel	+90 (252) 2842109
fax	+90 (252) 2842109
email	dalyan@happycaretta.com

Guest house

Map 4 Entry 97

Dalyan Hotel

Maraş Mah. Sağlık Sok. 9, 48840 Dalyan, Muğla

The position is fantastic, alone on a tongue of land jutting out into the Dalyan River directly opposite the soaring cliff and the Lycian royal tombs carved directly into the rock. Riverboats sail past all day long, swishing by the reeds at the edge of the garden. The circular swimming pool is surrounded by the river on three sides so you feel you are in a magic enclosure far removed from the town's rush and bustle. The bedrooms are basic, modern and somewhat unloved, and have river or tomb views. But then you are likely to spend much of the day outside – idling by the pool (floodlit at night), taking liquid refreshment at the riverside bar or riding the hotel boat for a leisurely sail down the river. There's also a daily shuttle to the beach. A predominantly English clientele continues to enjoy Dalyan Hotel into its twentieth year. Within boating distance is the endless labyrinth of Dalyan's delta, with its hot mud baths and the ruins of the ancient city of Caunus lying in desolate grandeur. The landscape is of unforgettable beauty.

rooms	20 twins/doubles.
price	Half board 150 YTL.
	Singles (half-board) 110 YTL.
meals	30-45 YTL, with wine.
closed	November-April.
directions	In Dalyan: downriver (left) at centre.
airport	27km from Dalaman Airport.

	Ünver Peker
tel	+90 (252) 2842239
fax	+90 (252) 2842240
email	info@hoteldalyan.com
web	www.hoteldalyan.com

Hotel

Map 4 Entry 98

Ottoman Residence

Gülpınar Mah. 751 Sok. 28, 48840 Dalyan, Muğla

This compound of self-catering holiday apartments, variously called Residence or Retreat, stands apart from the rest of the breed by virtue of its fine architecture – a modern vision of the traditional Ottoman house with projecting upper floors, executed with a fine sense of detail and excellent craftsmanship. The duplex apartments have sleek, simply-furnished modern interiors, simple shower rooms and all the conveniences one could wish for in a holiday home. They surround the meticulously clipped lawn that borders the classy swimming pool. Mr Peker is a retired ship's captain with all the charm and quiet humour of a seaman of the old school. His guests are mostly British families on holiday for a week at a time. The riverbank is a short walk down the street. A few years ago, this area north of the town used to be cornfields as far as the eye could see; now, the boxhouses of holiday compounds are spreading over those fields like an unstoppable prairie fire.

rooms	14 apartments: 10 for 2, 4 for 4.
price	Apts for 2, 130 YTL. Apts for 4, 220 YTL. Breakfast extra.
meals	Meals by arrangement.
closed	November–April.
directions	600m from Dalyan: turn right at centre; left at hotel sign, 300m.
airport	29km from Dalaman Airport.

	Taner Peker & Levent Yıldız
tel	+90 (252) 2844498
fax	+90 (252) 2844751
email	info@ottomanretreat.com
web	www.ottomanretreat.com

Self-catering

Map 4 Entry 99

Sultan Palace

(PK 10), 48840 Dalyan, Muğla

The position of this hotel is perfect if you want to keep well away from the beach-and-beer crowds of summertime Dalyan: you have to cross the river by boat to the uninhabited right bank, then walk one small kilometre along cornfields and heathland to reach what looks, from a distance, like a smallish castle with a round turret. The forested hills rise behind and there's not another dwelling within sight. The silence is overwhelming. The hotel dates from the early 1980s. The buildings show their age a little although the rooms have undergone a recent overhaul and been fitted with much-needed air-conditioning. More memorable is the vast and peaceful garden that surrounds the swimming pool. Dinner, a generous buffet of Turkish and European specialties, is laid out by the pool for a predominantly English clientele. The renowned mudbaths of Dalyan, where you can enjoy the unusual spectacle of several hundred half-naked tourists wallowing in black slime, are to be found 600 metres along this bank.

rooms	26 suites.
price	Half board 140 YTL. Singles 80 YTL.
meals	Half board only.
closed	November–April.
directions	4km from Dalyan: left at Ortaca/Köyceğiz junction, cross river to western bank (boat access only). Alternative road from Köyceğiz via Sultaniye.
airport	29km from Dalaman Airport.

	Nilgün Öztürk
tel	+90 (252) 2842103
fax	+90 (252) 2842106
email	sultanpalas@hotmail.com

Hotel

Map 4 Entry 100

Villa Gökbel
Gökbel, 48840 Dalyan, Muğla

A quiet, pleasant littlel hotel in a farming village far removed from the overcharged tourist-trap world of Dalyan, Villa Gökbel is the only accommodation of any sort in the village. It overlooks the extraordinary panorama of the delta, a vast labyrinth of swamps and lagoons surrounded by abrupt mountains, and is only a short drive from the great unspoilt beach of İztuzu where the giant loggerhead turtles frolic in summer. Your host is a gentleman with an academic background who originally built a summer home here and on second thoughts became a hotel-keeper. His is a friendly and informal establishment with a comfortable lounge, a big fireplace, a well-stocked bar and good cuisine at dinner. (There no other place to eat in the village, though Dalyan is only eight kilometres away by car.) Bedrooms and shower rooms of varying shapes and sizes have all mod cons. A great rock and an ancient carob tree dominate the garden; an olive tree grows out of one guest bathroom; the swimming pool seems to float off the edge of the rock into the void.

rooms	6 twins/doubles.
price	100 YTL. Singles 60 YTL.
meals	30-45 YTL, with wine.
closed	November-April.
directions	8km from Dalyan: İztuzu beach road.
airport	40km from Dalaman Airport.

	A. Arslan Türkoğul
tel	+90 (252) 2890046
fax	+90 (252) 2890047
email	aat@ada.net.tr
web	www.villagokbel.com

Hotel

Map 4 Entry 101

Kashmir Boutique Hotel

Kavakarası, 48800 Köyceğiz, Muğla

The private driveway that coils through the park-like forest might well lead to a serious French château. The farmhouse is neither French nor château but a reasonable substitute as far as the modern world is concerned: opulent, with vast grounds and utterly alone in a secluded o farming property of heaven knows how many acres. Lawns, ambitious water features, experimental hothouses and orchards stretch as far as the eye can see; forest protects the outer reaches. The farm was originally designed to grow carnations for large-scale export; then it hosted a high-gloss television serial. Now a hotel, it retains the atmosphere of a private, intimate country club. The owner is a well-known textile manufacturer who delights in playing host himself. There is a palatial suite with private dining room, library and fireplace, and two suites have living rooms, but every room is dapper. Fine meals, Turkish wines, a duck-paddled stream, two swimming pools – this is a treat for families. *Closed summer 2005 pending construction of new 16-room unit.*

rooms	6: 3 twins/doubles, 3 suites.
price	140 YTL. Suites 230 YTL. Singles 110 YTL.
meals	30-45 YTL, with wine.
closed	Never.
directions	12km from Köyceğiz: Dalaman road 11km, right on the 'old' Dalyan road.
airport	24km from Dalaman Airport.

Mustafa Adanır

tel	+90 (252) 2648187
fax	+90 (252) 2648247
email	info@kashmirtourism.net
web	www.kashmirtourism.net

Hotel

Map 4 Entry 102

Garden Eden Motel

Sultaniye, 48800 Köyceğiz, Muğla

The road to Ekincik is one of the most beautiful stretches of southwestern Turkey. The land is mountainous and fertile, and Lake Köyceğiz is of dreamlike beauty on its uninhabited West coast. Garden Eden (sic!) slumbers under a gigantic plane tree on the outskirts of the lush little village of Sultaniye, half way down this road. Sultaniye is famous mainly for its historic baths, which stand grimy and neglected on the edge of the lake. Visitors usually arrive by boat from Dalyan. They sometimes walk over to have lunch at Garden Eden, which is the only establishment of any sort in the village. Some of them even travel all the way from Dalyan to spend the day slumbering in a hammock under the thick shade of the plane tree. The pension is a modest one with ten quite basic, if meticulously clean and bright rooms. Mr Yıldız and his family run the place with a lot of charm. There is a small swimming pool. The surroundings are overwhelmingly quiet and the orchards and the woods around the village afford plenty of shady walks even during the hotter days of summer.

rooms	10 twins/doubles.
price	40 YTL. Singles 30 YTL.
meals	20-30 YTL.
closed	Occasionally in winter.
directions	24km from Köyceğiz: Ekincik road from either Köyceğiz or Döğüşbelen.
airport	65km from Dalaman Airport.

	Zihni Yıldız
tel	+90 (252) 2660140
fax	+90 (252) 2660140

Guest house

Map 4 Entry 103

Yonca's Retreat
Göcek, 48300 Fethiye, Muğla

A civilised and stylish little hotel tucked away with shy effacement in a back street of Göcek, Yonca's Retreat has more the atmosphere of a comfortable home or a private club than an ordinary hotel. Breakfast, for example, is of the kind that one saves for a much-loved guest on a Sunday morning and the cosy poolside bar invites leisurely hours in the shade of the big mulberry tree. The retreat's clients are almost all English, as are a large proportion of the visitors and the expatriates of this quiet harbour village in the Gulf of Fethiye. Each of the eight rooms is furnished with carefully chosen antiques that reflect Mrs Arsal's background as an antique dealer in Istanbul's fashionable Nişantaşı district. Mr Arsal is a yacht builder who left the big city to settle in this the mecca of Turkey's sailing enthusiasts, then went into the hotel business to remedy an old adage that there was no place to stay in Göcek except at sea. He keeps a sailing boat for the benefit of guests who wish to test that saying for themselves.

rooms	8 twins/doubles.
price	90 YTL. Singles 70 YTL.
meals	Restaurants nearby.
closed	November-March.
directions	In Göcek: inland.
airport	25km from Dalaman Airport.

	Yonca & Tolon Arsal
tel	+90 (252) 6452255
fax	+90 (252) 6452275
email	yoncaresort@superonline.com

Hotel

Map 4 Entry 104

A&B Home Hotel
Turgut Özal Cad., Göcek, 48300 Fethiye, Muğla

A is for Ayşe, who is no longer here. B is for Birkan, a great hulk of a man who seems to delight every one of his guests with his relaxed, slightly bumbling hospitality. He started out as an engineer in the yuppielands of Istanbul, then became a yacht captain and subsequently decided to settle in Göcek, the sailing capital of the Turkish Riviera. His spit-and-polish Harley-Davidson stands at the gate of his hotel on the main street of Göcek, an uncrowded, pleasant thoroughfare lined with good pubs and fancy antique shops. There is a bijou pool in the front yard, good enough for a daily dip, and a café-bar where you can grab a quick lunch and a beer. Rooms are functional and supplied with all basic comforts like a good solid bed and a hair dryer. Breakfast is a colourful spread – six homemade jams and two kinds of eggs – and the harbour is two blocks away. This is a convenient place to spend a couple of days before or after a sailing excursion, as you run through the boating arrangements or wait for that 6am flight out of Dalaman airport.

rooms	11 twins/doubles.
price	95 YTL. Singles 75 YTL.
meals	Meals by arrangement.
closed	Never.
directions	In Göcek: on the main street.
airport	25km from Dalaman Airport.

	Birkan Çetiner
tel	+90 (252) 6451820
fax	+90 (252) 6451843
email	birkan@abhomehotel.com
web	www.abhomehotel.com

Hotel

Map 4 Entry 105

Montenegro

Gökçeovacık, 48300 Fethiye, Muğla

When Mr Karadağ decided to leave the city and settle in the mountains, he brought with him his social habits, his music (Buddha Bar, Nirvana), his cigars and his brand-conscious glasses. His hotel is a bracket of civility set in the wilderness of the high Taurus Mountains. The setting is timeless: there are scraggy limestone cliffs all around, a small village where coffee-house talk is about the olive press or the goat exchange, a pine forest in the background and cactus growing wild out of the red rocky soil. Yet it is only a 15-minute drive down to Göcek, the sophisticated yachties' favourite haven. The establishment has two parts. There is the hotel itself, whose six low-lying rooms surround a tranquil swimming pool. A few steps lower down are two self-catering cottages designed for longer-term guests. Outwardly they give the appearance of ancient simplicity: they are built of the local stone and sit in a beautiful precision-crafted garden. Inside, they are in a contemporary style and touched by the newest technology.

rooms	6 + 3: 6 twins/doubles. 2 cottages for 3, 1 cottage for 6.
price	210 YTL. Cottages for 3, 360 YTL. Cottages for 6, 500 YTL.
meals	45-60 YTL, with wine.
closed	November-April.
directions	9km from Göcek: Fethiye road 2km, left to Gökçeovacık, then through village for further 2km.
airport	33km from Dalaman Airport.

	Selim Karadağ
tel	+90 (252) 6440181
fax	+90 (252) 6440182
email	selim.karadag@teklan.com.tr
web	www.montenegro.com.tr

Hotel & Self-catering

Map 4 Entry 106

Ocakköy

Ovacık Mvk, Ölüdeniz, 48300 Fethiye, Muğla

A holiday complex designed with modesty and love, Ocakköy stands on a broad hillside behind a pine forest, far from the loud commercialism of the Fethiye and Ölüdeniz resorts. Built around the ruins of a medieval hamlet that was abandoned a century ago, its stone cottages, surrounded by flower-filled patios and cultivated vegetable patches, replicate the originals. The picture-perfect beach of Ölüdeniz (best out of season) lies five kilometres and a free weekday shuttle away. The idea was born 25 years ago when a handful of Germans and Englishmen – a businessman, a professor, a photographer – met by chance in Ölüdeniz and fell in love with the place. They resisted the logic of mass tourism, which has transformed the neighbouring villages from rustic backwater into boomtown, and combined traditional materials and crafts with modern comforts for a great, authentic feel. Most guests are English and part of the resort is set aside for the disabled who can enjoy all Ocakköy's facilities with ease. There are two pools, several bars and a fair bit of uncluttered land to spread on.

rooms	44 + 30: 14 twins/doubles. 15 cottages for 2, 15 cottages for 4.
price	60 YTL. Singles 45 YTL. Cottages for 4, 100 YTL. Breakfast extra.
meals	30-45 YTL, with wine.
closed	November-April.
directions	7km from Fethiye: Ölüdeniz road, right (marked) into forest track immed. after mountain pass.
airport	56km from Dalaman Airport.

	Friedrich W Schmidt & Eda Tuna
tel	+90 (252) 6166156
fax	+90 (252) 6166158
email	ocakkoy@superonline.com

Hotel & Self-catering

Map 4 Entry 107

Paradise Garden

Belcekız Mvk., Ölüdeniz, 48300 Fethiye, Muğla

This is one of the most extraordinary gardens of all Turkey. Spread over a 15-acre swathe of steep hillside, it is a strange and spontaneous labyrinth of meticulously planted patches, hidden alcoves and grand and flawed projects left mostly half-finished. Hidden in it are a vast aviary, a collection of hybrid citrus species and three large swimming pools one of which is dug into a cave. A breathtaking view of the gorge of Ölüdeniz spreads under the feet. The god of this quirky paradise is Mr Gürsu, a former tour operator and entrepreneur who devoted excess energy from a business career that had been filled with spectacular ups and downs to cultivating his garden. The hotel itself started as an afterthought. The building is unexciting in comparison to the garden, though perfectly comfortable and sanely furnished. It is run by a remarkably charming young manager who directs a staff that is as quirky and unpredictable as the boss himself. The beach of Ölüdeniz, one of the most beautiful in the entire Mediterranean and unfortunately known as such, is three kilometres away.

rooms	26: 24 twins/doubles, 2 suites.
price	180 YTL-210 YTL. Suites 225 YTL. Singles from 140 YTL.
meals	45-60 YTL, with wine.
closed	December-March.
directions	2km from Ölüdeniz: off the Fethiye road, at the highest point.
airport	60km from Dalaman Airport.

Öncü Gürsu

tel	+90 (252) 6170545
fax	+90 (252) 6170544
email	info@paradisegardenhotel.com
web	www.paradisegardenhotel.com

Hotel

Map 4 Entry 108

Oyster Residences/Ölüdeniz

Belcekız Sok. 1, Ölüdeniz, 48300 Fethiye, Muğla

We would not have imagined that a really nice small hotel could exist in the beachtown jumble of Ölüdeniz-village. As of 2004, one does. Its creator is Mehmet Günel, the man who brought you Oyster Residence at Faralya and the fabulous White Dolphin Restaurant. What is striking is that a hotel so new could actually convey the looks and textures of an elegant house from the good old times. The wide floorboards, lovely oak furniture and classically proportioned windows, all seem to belong more to 1904 than 2004. Rooms are furnished sparsely and in good taste, their softly-draped French windows leading to a tree-shaded garden. Despite the limited space, the overall feeling is remarkably quiet and cool. A large swimming pool occupies part of the garden; the beach – a mile-long stretch of heavenly whitish sand – is just outside. In the magnificent setting of the tall mountains and placid lagoon, one can only try to imagine that once just a couple of modest camping sites existed where today some 40 hotels and twice as many restaurants vie for attention.

rooms	16 twins/doubles.
price	200 YTL. Singles 150 YTL.
meals	45-60 YTL, with wine.
closed	November-April.
directions	In Ölüdeniz: off beachfront.
airport	62km from Dalaman Airport.

	Günsenin Günel
tel	+90 (252) 6170765
fax	+90 (252) 6170764
email	oludeniz@oysterresidences.com
web	www.oysterresidences.com

Hotel

Map 4 Entry 109

Su Değirmeni

Hisar Mah. 4, Uzunyurt (Faralya), 48300 Fethiye, Muğla

Beyond Ölüdeniz starts one of Turkey's last remaining stretches of virgin coast. The road climbs to prodigious heights along the corniche, passing scattered farms and hamlets where a tourist still arouses the curiosity of the children. Below a precipice is the Valley of Butterflies, its unspoilt beach nearly impossible to reach from land. Değirmen (meaning 'watermill') clings to a crevice of the mountain above the valley. It is a comfortable and civilised retreat built of stone and timber on sound ecological principles; hot water and heating are solar powered and a quiet pool is maintained by non-chemical means. Bread is wholemeal and organic, fruits and veg fresh from the garden, afternoon cakes are delicious. The rooms may be vast but are cosily outfitted with fireplaces and kilims and smell of fresh pine; most have balconies and fantastic views. Suites, with sofabeds and 'tea kitchens', sleep four. The Lycian Trail leads up from the mill to the ruins of Sidyma, a three-hour hike. Ferruh and Brigitte are willing hosts to a predominantly German clientele of nature and outdoor enthusiasts.

rooms	8: 2 twins/doubles, 6 suites for 4.
price	Half board 130 YTL. Suites 190 YTL. Singles from 65 YTL.
meals	Half board only.
closed	November-March.
directions	8km from Ölüdeniz: south past Lycia World, first cluster of houses after the great cliff, poorly marked.
airport	72km from Dalaman Airport.

	Brigitte & Ferruh Özbalı
tel	+90 (252) 6421245
fax	+90 (252) 6421179
email	info@natur-reisen.de
web	www.natur-reisen.de

Hotel

Map 4 Entry 110

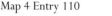

Oyster Residences/Faralya
Uzunyurt (Faralya), 48300 Fethiye, Muğla

Having travelled to the ends of the earth, Mehmet Günel has learnt the first lesson of travelling which is: avoid luggage! Oyster Faralya is a masterpiece of simplicity. It enchants by its intelligent modesty as much as its dramatic location. It feels like the end of the world. You drive a terrifying rut down the cliff of Faralya to reach the bottom of the rock where an attractive garden lies perfectly isolated at the edge of the sea. The setting is pure Mediterranean — limestone rock, crooked pines and centuries-old olive trees. The modest and secluded cabins offer all the comforts that count: a canopied bed, sometimes a second bed on the terrace in case you want to sleep outside, sheets of the whitest linen, fresh flowers on the table, plenty of wood for the fireplace. A wood-burning samovar supplies fresh tea all day long and you can breakfast whenever you like. A great asset is İsmail, the perfect butler who has found his life's happiness in this place of utter isolation. He serves gourmet-class food and knows the secret of pampering a guest without appearing to do much.

rooms	6 twins/doubles.
price	Half board 300 YTL.
meals	Half board only.
closed	Never.
directions	14km from Ölüdeniz: south past Lycia World and Uzunyurt, right at white-painted pole (no sign, poor road).
airport	78km from Dalaman Airport.

	İsmail Çullar
tel	+90 (252) 6170765
fax	+90 (252) 6170764
email	faralya@oysterresidences.com
web	www.oysterresidences.com

Guest house

Map 4 Entry 111

Kabak Natural Life

Kabak Mvk., Uzunyurt (Faralya), 48300 Fethiye, Muğla

South of Ölüdeniz, the road continues for some way, curving dizzily along the mountain flank and coming to an end at the hamlet of Kabak. Kabak (which can mean either Bald or Pumpkin) hangs on the rock about 300 metres above the sea. From here, a 20-minute hike down a mountain path will bring the unsuspecting traveller to a different world, the Liberated Republic of Kabak's Kampsites. There are four or five camping sites in all, grouped close together at the bottom of the lushly overgrown valley. Best-known among them is Natural Life, run by a well-travelled (and well-read) pair of professional nature photographers and frequented by a highly international clientele of the environment-conscious, yoga-practising, vegetarian sort. The accommodations are primitive – tent, thatched cabin, tree house and hammock – but the food is good and one should not be surprised to find tomes of Nietzsche in the camp library. A short walk along the valley brings you to a dazzling beach of fine sand, utterly isolated and beautiful.

rooms	17 cabins with shared showers.
price	Half board 90 YTL.
meals	Half board only.
closed	November–March.
directions	20km from Ölüdeniz: south past Uzunyurt/Faralya to the end of the road at Kabak. Walk 20 min downhill.
airport	85km from Dalaman Airport.

	Levent & Nilüfer Akat
tel	+90 (252) 6421181
email	info@kabaknaturallife.com
web	www.kabakcamping.com

Camp

Map 4 Entry 112

Mountain Lodge
Yaka (Tlos), 48300 Fethiye, Muğla

A charming English pub and B&B lost in a faraway, little-known village in mountainous Lycia. Young Mel and Mick worked tooth and nail to build their dream cottage here. They opened two lovingly furnished rooms to guests, then added some more. Then they took a major step towards professionalism by building a few comfortable houses with bigger, better, English-style carpeted rooms. They serve pub food as well as Turkish classics, have a nice garden, a swimming pool, a relaxed atmosphere and a lot of good humour. Mick guides hiking tours into the further recesses of the mountains; he climbs the rocks and instructs paragliders. Two little daughters round up the team. It's the sort of place where one drops by for a beer and ends up staying for a week. A short stroll up the hill is the great rock of Tlos, pockmarked with the carved tombs of the ancient Lycians and crowned with the ruined stronghold of an 18th-century robber baron. The carcass of a Roman bathhouse lies near the toppled theatre. They command a sweeping view of almost all of western Lycia.

rooms	8: 7 twins/doubles, 1 suite.
price	70-100 YTL. Singles from 35 YTL.
meals	20-30 YTL.
closed	Never.
directions	30km from Fethiye: Korkuteli road 24km; right shortly after Kaş junction; left in Güneşli, 3km to Yaka/Tlos.
airport	85km from Dalaman Airport.

	Mel & Mick Scarsbrook
tel	+90 (252) 6382515
fax	+90 (252) 6382220
email	mlodge@atlas.net.tr
web	www.themountainlodge.co.uk

Guest house

Map 4 Entry 113

Berg Hof

Yaka (Tlos), 48300 Fethiye, Muğla

A hill retreat of very German spirit lost in an unlikely corner of the Lycian countryside. The owners are a retired German couple who fell in love with this piece of wild southern mountain and proceeded to build the home they had been longing for. The property is huge, wooded and well-ordered, protected by high gates and German shepherd dogs. It is above all very quiet. The swimming pool lies utterly solitary at the edge of a forested valley and commands a superb view of the Eşen Plain. The rooms, by contrast, are quite simple and with no particular character. Frau Kochs now runs the place by herself, and even insists on cooking in person when people ask for meals. The village itself is idyllic. It lies at the foot of a hill pitted with ancient Lycian rock tombs and capped with a medieval fortress. The ruin of a splendid Roman bath lies buried in ivy. Further up the hill are some waterfalls and trout farms that have become popular with day-excursion groups from Fethiye. A decent alternative to the often-full Mountain Lodge.

rooms	4 twins/doubles.
price	70 YTL. Singles 35 YTL.
meals	Meals by arrangement.
closed	Never.
directions	30km from Fethiye: Korkuteli road 24km; right shortly after Kaş junction; left in Güneşli, 3 km to Yaka/Tlos.
airport	85km from Dalaman Airport.

	Brigitte Kochs
tel	+90 (252) 6382444
fax	+90 (252) 6382444
email	brigittekochs@hotmail.com

Guest house

Map 4 Entry 114

Tekkebaşı Dervish Lodge
Alınca Mvk., Karaağaç, 48300 Fethiye, Muğla

Avoid it if you worry about the smaller comforts of life, and don't even think of it if you are afraid of heights. If you enjoy adventure, however, it is the extremeness that makes this an exhilarating place. The location is the edge of a near-vertical 850-metre cliff looking over the sea. The road is mostly unpaved; it climbs in hairpin bends that will test the mettle of the toughest driver. Here, outside an archaic little village, a dervish – a mendicant saint – once had his lodge. His modern successor is a photographer who used to be editor of the country's leading travel mag. His hut sits by the Lycian Trail, a popular hiking route. There are a few relatively comfortable hut and cabin rooms with private (but external) bathrooms. Otherwise, you can sleep in a traditional tent, sling a hammock, or do as the locals do and sleep on the flat roof of the stone cabin, facing the stars. You can walk down to the beach at Kabak in an hour. It is a two-hour panting and puffing climb back up – or a 80-km drive round the mountain via Ölüdeniz, Fethiye and Eşen.

rooms	7: 2 huts for 2, 3 cabins, 2 tents for 3, some with own showers.
price	Half board 100 YTL, cabins 80 YTL, tents 60 YTL.
meals	Half board only.
closed	December-February.
directions	61km from Fethiye: Kaş road for 45km, right to Boğaziçi, frightful road to Alınca/Karaağaç. No road access from Ölüdeniz.
airport	110km from Dalaman Airport.

	Erdem Yavaşça
tel	+90 (252) 6791142
web	www.dervishlodge.com

Camp

Map 4 Entry 115

Photo Nişanyan Gezi Tanitim Ltd, Selçuk, Turkey

mediterranean

coastal playground 2

The Taurus Mountains form a barrier between the southern coast and the plateau. The coast is spectacularly rugged to the west, where small harbours like Kalkan, Kaş and Kekova cling to rocky coves cradled by cliffs, and the Gulf of Antalya is fringed by a hundred miles of sandy beach.

The Mediterranean summer is virtually cloud-free, and winter brings enough rainfall to support lush, quasi-tropical flora. This was wild and primitive country within living memory. Now it has grown into the powerhouse of Turkish tourism, the destination of 10 million beach-seekers each summer.

The 'hotel coast' stretches almost unbroken from Kemer to Alanya. Except for the pretty Old Town of Antalya, and the odd other nook or cranny, this stretch of coast remains outside the scope of this book. The west, where the topography does not favour large-scale investment, is a different matter. Kalkan and Kaş are attractive small-scale towns, while Kekova and Olympos deserve to be listed among the most magical spots on earth.

The ruins of ancient Lycian towns stand in awesome and beautiful settings. Some — Arycanda, Olympos, Phaselis and Termessos among them — are popular. Others, like Phellos, Cyaneai, Aperlai and Tyrsa, are barely on the tourist map.

Fidanka Aparts

Kışla Mvk., 07960 Kalkan, Muğla

Kalkan abounds in well-furnished apartment flats or houses, geared mainly towards the English holiday market. Many take full advantage of the town's fabulous sea views from steep hillside locations. In summer – and increasingly during the off-season as well – the town turns into a predominantly English colony. Fidanka Houses stand a head above the many similar establishments offering holiday rooms in Kalkan. The site, in a newly developed section to the east of the town, may be less than perfect, but the layout of the property is very pleasant, with eight generously sized units hugging a beautiful swimming pool. The apartments are decorated elegantly, in part with valuable antiques, and each comes with a living room, kitchen and private terrace. The garden is a riot of flowers, the handiwork of Nükhet Hanım, a charming lady from Istanbul who owns and runs the place with her two daughters and their families. A 300-metre walk down the hill is the beach, where you can dive from rock platforms into the fabulously clear and deep sea.

rooms	8 apartments: 6 for 2, 2 for 4.
price	Apts for 2, 105-115 YTL. Apts for 4, 175 YTL.
meals	30-45 YTL, with wine.
closed	15th November-March.
directions	2km from Kalkan: Kaş road, right at Club Patara, 200m on left.
airport	120km from Dalaman Airport.

	Evrim & Bilge Bayer, Cüneyt Vatan
tel	+90 (242) 8441245
fax	+90 (242) 8441200
email	evrimbayer@superonline.com
web	www.fidanka.com

Self-catering

Map 4 Entry 116

Villa Mahal

PK 4, 07960 Kalkan, Antalya

The cliff-top position is breathtaking. You look down on the deep indigo of the bay of Kalkan's from a height of more than 180 steps. The buildings, bright white and Mediterranean blue, hunker down against the earth in their sun-drenched olive grove so that you scarcely see them. Impeccable rooms come in various shapes and sizes: there are deluxe ones with private terraces and several private suites set in wonderfully secluded corners. At the top end is the Pool Suite, with its own infinity pool (see photo) suspended between the bedroom and the void. The view is bewitching at night as the lights of Kalkan glitter in the distance. Way below is the sea with a swimming platform over the rocks and a bar-restaurant where one can loll about all day long. The style is civilised and unobtrusive, mixing touches of class with a casual beach tone; sumptuous dinners and breakfasts are also served on the rooftop terrace. Above all, it is very private: reclinging on your terrace, you may forget that there is any hotel around you at all. *Children nine and over welcome.*

rooms	14: 11 twins/doubles, 3 suites.
price	230 YTL. Suites 320-390 YTL. Singles from 210 YTL.
meals	45-60 YTL, with wine.
closed	November-March.
directions	2km from Kalkan: Kaş road; right at Club Patara.
airport	120km from Dalaman Airport.

	İpek Tolbas
tel	+90 (242) 8443268
fax	+90 (242) 8442122
email	villamahal@turk.net
web	www.villamahal.com

Hotel

Map 4 Entry 117

Owlsland

Bezirgân, 07960 Kalkan, Antalya

Here is a happy marriage of good Scottish taste and unspoilt Turkish highlander spirit. Erol and Pauline retreated up the hill to this mountain village after running a highly regarded restaurant in Kalkan. Their guest house is a delightful 150-year-old that has been repaired with modesty and skill; it oozes charm and simple, practical comforts. Under the pergola of grapevine, which looks as if it hasn't ever changed, we were served ginger biscuits and Ceylon tea in fine English china. For delicious breakfast there's honey from the family's bees, local eggs and homemade jams. The furniture is hand-made from cedar wood and there is a herb garden full of very un-Turkish species. Bezirgan village is a modest Shangri-La set in an enclosed dip in the Taurus Mountains, 1,000 metres *straight* up from the sea; it is hard to imagine so unspoilt and 'real' a village this close to the doctored charms of Kalkan. At night, you can sit out in a thick sweater on the cosily-cushioned balcony and watch the stars on high as they shine with unreal brightness because there are no other lights to compete.

rooms	3 twins/doubles.
price	95 YTL. Singles 45 YTL.
meals	Meals by arrangement.
closed	15 November–15 February.
directions	17km from Kalkan: 1km toward Fethiye, right marked Bezirgan/Elmali.
airport	135km from Dalaman Airport.

	Pauline & Erol Şalvarlı
tel	+90 (242) 8375214
email	owlsland@superonline.com
web	www.owlsland.com

Guest house

Map 4 Entry 118

Hadrian Hotel

Çukurbağ Yarımadası, 07580 Kaş, Antalya

A bright, modern, comfortable hotel that clings to the edge of the rock at the far end of Çukurbağ Peninsula, a four-kilometre-long spit of rock off the west side of the attractive harbour of Kaş. The sea is all around you, dazzling in its deep rich colour. Like all other buildings that are part of the peninsula's planned development, Hadrian is built in low blocks that approximate the traditional style of Kaş houses. The sunny courtyard, covered by heaps of purple bougainvillea, exploits the position to full panoramic effect and has a large, classy-curvy swimming pool in the middle that serves as the focal point of social life. A platform on the rocky ledge gives access to the sea, which is very deep and well-suited for snorkelling and diving. The energetic Mr Kızılkaya and his German wife create a hospitable and informal atmosphere for their guests. Activities include boat trips and excursions into the Taurus mountains.

rooms	14: 10 twins/doubles, 4 suites.
price	Half board 150-170 YTL. Suites 210 YTL. Singles from 95 YTL.
meals	Half board only.
closed	15 November-April.
directions	6km from Kaş: turn right in Kaş centre for Çukurbağ peninsula.
airport	160km from Dalaman Airport.

Ursula & Tamer Kızılkaya
tel   +90 (242) 8362856
fax   +90 (242) 8361387
email   info@hotel-hadrian.de
web   www.hotel-hadrian.de

Hotel

Map 4 Entry 119

Aquarius Hotel

Çukurbağ Yarımadası, 07580 Kaş, Antalya

Aquarius stands out among the two dozen quasi-identical hotels of the Çukurbağ peninsula on two counts – firstly, for the exceptional charm and friendliness of the management, and secondly, for the best private beach by far and wide. The latter is in fact a rock platform like every other 'beach' in this spectacularly rocky land, though it does enjoy – along with only one other beach within 150 miles – the Blue Flag that the European Environmental Union awards to beaches of outstanding quality. The rooms are comfortable and clean if rather small and the food is a good notch above average hotel standard. The Greek island of Castellorizo is a mere 1.5 miles from the Turkish coast at this point – a tiny outpost of Greece lying some 80 miles from the nearest Greek territory. Its harbour is probably the cutest of all Greek islands, a stage set of gaily painted houses and tavernas serving a population of 200.

rooms	32: 28 twins/doubles, 4 suites for 4.
price	Half board 140 YTL. Suites 175 YTL. Singles 105 YTL.
meals	Half board only.
closed	November-15 May.
directions	6km from Kaş: turn right in Kaş centre for Çukurbağ peninsula.
airport	160km from Dalaman Airport.

	Kenan Yanıkbaca
tel	+90 (242) 8361896
fax	+90 (242) 8362021
email	info@hotelaquarius.net
web	www.hotelaquarius.net

Hotel

Map 4 Entry 120

Nesrin's Bademli Ev

Kale Üçağız, 07570 Demre, Antalya

This is the perfect Mediterranean dream: a sun-drenched cottage with a good sea view, hosted by a charming multilingual lady who is conversant with the classics (her late husband was a professor of Latin) and serves the perfect breakfast with real silver cutlery. The house has metre-thick stone walls that may be 100 or 1,000 years old, ceilings of ancient timber and a fireplace in each whitewashed room. There is a creaky wooden terrace where you can sit in utter peace – the village of Kale/Simena has no motor vehicles – and watch the ever-changing colours of the harbour. Or you can relax under the eucalyptus tree in the shade of a massive rock that turns out on closer inspection to be a Lycian house-tomb. A few twists of crooked village lane bring you down to the waterfront where there is a string of fishermen's restaurants, and rowing boats that you can borrow to explore in solitude the sunken ruins of a Lycian city which perished in an earthquake 2,060 years ago. Feast on Nesrin's jams at breakfast; dine at one of those restaurants by the sea.

rooms	3 twins/doubles.
price	From 80 YTL.
meals	Restaurants nearby.
closed	November–April.
directions	31km from Kaş: road to Üçağız, then take boat (10 mins); no road access to Kale village.
airport	140km from Antalya Airport.

	Nesrin Demircioğlu
tel	+90 (242) 8742170
fax	+90 (242) 8742093
email	askatech@ada.net.tr
web	www.askamarine.com/bademliev.htm

Guest house

Map 4 Entry 121

Kale Pansiyon

Kale Üçağız, 07570 Demre, Antalya

A place for total escape. This is a basic, family-run *pansiyon* at the edge of the sea in the archaic village of Kale, sprinkled with sea salt and so completely enmeshed with Lycian antiquities that it is impossible to tell which bit of masonry is two millennia old and which bit was built last year. The absence of motor traffic works its magic: street and courtyard blend together and the whole village sometimes gives the feeling of being one large cosy living room. The sea is as close as it gets: between your rustic bedroom and your breakfast table there are boats bobbing on the water. How so? The family pier, which gets longer and wider by the year, carries the family restaurant where you can sit with a glass of beer and watch your dinner being plucked from the net. There's also an ancient fisherman's cottage to rent, with a small garden and a stunning view. By day, the tour boats from Kaş and Demre cause some havoc; at night it becomes pure magic again, with no more than a few dozen outsiders left in the village, and the bay of Kekova turns into an exotic and closed world.

rooms	11: 10 twins/doubles, 1 cottage for 2.
price	90 YTL. Singles 50 YTL. Cottage 90 YTL.
meals	30-45 YTL, with wine.
closed	November-April.
directions	31km from Kaş: road to Üçağız, then take boat (10 mins); no road access to Kale village.
airport	140km from Antalya Airport.

	Salih Can
tel	+90 (242) 8742111
fax	+90 (242) 8742110
email	kalepansiyon@ixir.com
web	www.kalepansiyon.com

Guest house

Map 4 Entry 122

Mehtap Pansiyon
Kale Üçağız, 07570 Demre, Antalya

Our third selection in the fantastic village of Kale/Simena is set in the upper part of the village. You have to climb down almost 100 metres to reach the sea – and back up again to come home – but the bonus is an eerily beautiful panorama over the village rooftops and the sea. Directly below is the Sunken Tomb, standing in the sea like a mysterious treasure-chest, which lights up with a surreal light at sunset. İrfan and his wife serve their guests with stoic grace despite the personal tragedies that have struck their family quite recently. Their restaurant, spread over wooden platforms, makes the best of the catch of the day – and the fabulous views. The establishment is very basic and the bedrooms have few frills, though they are clean and have metre-thick stone walls that keep the summer heat at bay (air conditioning too). And... your neighbours on either side are two of the wealthiest men in Turkey, who have discovered in Kekova the most perfectly beautiful getaway there is in the whole country.

rooms	10 triples.
price	Half board 120 YTL. Singles 95 YTL.
meals	Half board only.
closed	Occasionally in winter.
directions	31km from Kaş: road to Üçağız, then boat (10 min); no road access to Kale village.
airport	140km from Antalya Airport.

İrfan Tezcan

tel	+90 (242) 8742146
fax	+90 (242) 8742261
email	info@mehtappansiyon.com
web	www.mehtappansiyon.com

Guest house

Map 4 Entry 123

Ankh Pansiyon
Kale Üçağız, 07570 Demre, Antalya

Ankh is a modest family-run guest house in the storybook village of Kale. The sea is literally at your doorstep: you walk out of your room onto a narrow platform wide enough for about 10 sunbathers and two hammocks and dip into the ever-brilliant waters of the Bay of Kekova. There is a rowing boat you can borrow to explore the sunken ruins of ancient Simena. Or you can lounge about the restaurant which doubles as the friendly Takır family's sitting room. There is fresh fish as usual; more unusual are the delicious homemade ice creams. The older rooms, made of concrete, are pretty basic, but the newer ones built in wood and pine-clad, are quite wide and airy. The village is topped with a medieval castle and is accessible only by sea. Scores of very small islets, some bearing hermits' cells and other mysterious ruined structures, are scattered across the harbour. Surrounded by the mountains, hardly touched by the modern world – give or take the odd yacht or two – this is as enchanting a site as there can be.

rooms	9 twins/doubles.
price	90 YTL. Singles 60 YTL.
meals	30-45 YTL, with wine.
closed	15 November-March.
directions	31km from Kaş: road to Üçağız, then boat (10 min); no road access to Kale village.
airport	140km from Antalya Airport.

	Ahmet & Hasan Takır
tel	+90 (242) 8742171
fax	+90 (242) 8742147
email	ankhcafepansion@superonline.com
web	www.ankhpansion.com

Guest house

Map 4 Entry 124

Onuncu Köy/Künstlerhof

PK 6, Çavuşköy (Adrasan), 07370 Kumluca, Antalya

A multinational artistic commune with a strongly, though by no means exclusively, German accent and a red-green political hue. The modest but attractive living quarters have been individually furnished by members, most of whom are Germans of a creative or academic bent, and allocated on a kind of timeshare system. Outsiders are welcome, too, so long as they share the cultural and political predilections of the fraternity. The commune, set among the cotton fields a 20-minute walk inland from Adrasan's splendid beach, also has a good big swimming pool and a restaurant that is usually excellent. Views reach beyond the lemon groves and vegetable gardens to the mountains, snow-capped till June. A Turkish proverb contends that a man who speaks the truth shall be kicked out of nine villages; the Ünal brothers had their share of being kicked around during the terrible reign of hypocrisy that swept this country after the military putsch of 1980. Tenth Village (Onuncu Köy) is their name for this brilliantly quixotic enterprise.

rooms	16: 8 twins/doubles, 8 suites for 4.
price	Half board 110 YTL. Singles 55 YTL.
meals	Half board only.
closed	15 November–15 March.
directions	12km from Olimpos: turn right on the way to Adrasan beach.
airport	106km from Antalya Airport.

	Halit Ünal
tel	+90 (242) 8831253
fax	+90 (242) 8831297
email	onuncukoy_kuenstlerhof@hotmail.com
web	www.kuenstlerhofadrasan.de

Guest house

Map 5 Entry 125

Eviniz

Deniz Cad. 540, Çavuşköy (Adrasan), 07370 Kumluca, Antalya

A quiet, pleasant and very proper, family-oriented guest house that carries central European *gemütlichkeit* into the searing Mediterranean sun. The owners are a retired German-Turkish couple who come from backgrounds in Heidelberg and Istanbul. Their garden is always well tended, their turquoise swimming pool sparkles under the umbrella pines, their rooms are free of all superfluous details but have light, balconies with sea views, the essential pine furniture and good bedding (some have air conditiioning and most can take extra beds). The cooking combines the very best of Turkish and German home styles and their presentation of dinner is exquisite. The name says it all: Eviniz means, more or less, 'Home Sweet Home'. Of all the beach towns of Turkey's Mediterranean shore, Adrasan remains one of the least touristy and the most village-like. Some of the spectacularly rugged ridges of the Taurus engulf the small beach-fringed basin: it was practically inaccessible by road until the 1980s.

rooms	8 twins/doubles.
price	Half board 120 YTL. Singles 90 YTL.
meals	Half board only.
closed	15 October–15 May.
directions	12km from Olimpos: use Olimpos exit from highway, continue to Adrasan, turn right on beach road.
airport	106km from Antalya Airport.

	Behzar & Ernst Beierle
tel	+90 (242) 8831110
fax	+90 (242) 8831086
email	beierle@superonline.com
web	www.eviniz.net

Guest house

Map 5 Entry 126

Kadir's Tree House Hotel

Yazır (Olimpos), 07350 Kumluca, Antalya

A cross between a jungle camp and a Taurus nomad summer settlement, built
with imagination and a great sense of humour, Kadir's Tree House Hotel consists
of huts of various shapes and sizes clapped together from timber and other
assorted materials. Some are perched high on great umbrella pines, others sit on
the ground – or even in a beached boat, Noah's-ark style. There are also semi-
covered platforms for sleeping bags and camping space for tents. The setting is
wonderful: in deep forest, beside a cool brook at the foot of the Taurus
mountains. The site has the standing of a legend within the international
backpacking fraternity, and Kadir's is repeatedly voted one of the world's
grooviest places to stay. Crowds of 200 are not unusual in August, although things
are quieter at other times. The staff consists mostly of volunteers from all
countries who work their way to earn their room, and inexpensive vegetarian
food is served all day long. The beach is a mile walk through the forest-engulfed
ruins of Olympus, and your hosts organise all sorts of adventures.

rooms	85: 45 cabins for 2-3, 40 tree houses for 2-4, some with own shower.
price	Half board cabins from 40 YTL. Tree houses 50 YTL. Singles from 30 YTL.
meals	Half board only.
closed	Never.
directions	35km from Kemer: use Olimpos exit, on the way to the ruins.
airport	92km from Antalya Airport.

	Kadir Kaya
tel	+90 (242) 8921250
fax	+90 (242) 8921110
email	treehouse@superonline.com
web	www.kadirstreehouses.com

Camp

Map 5 Entry 127

Daphne House
Yazır (Olimpos), 07350 Kumluca, Antalya

An immensely friendly, unpretentious guest house with a huge unkempt garden set under the shady canopy of a great pine forest. The owners are a young couple who drifted after university into the easy-going fraternity of Olympus and then, unlike others who moved on, decided to settle down and grow roots here. They built their house with their own hands, then expanded with a small guest house in the garden. They offer delightful, heartfelt hospitality to a highly international circle of guests. The cooking is mostly vegetarian and all the more deliciously varied in that guests often lend a helping hand. A guitar and a computer are essential elements of the facilities. The house stands two kilometres inland from the beach at the head of a beautiful walking trail and, moreover, Bülent is an excellent guide to the mountain trails of Lycia. The inland side of the forest-engulfed ruins of Olympus – the area called Olimpos proper, as opposed to Çıralı – is buried deep in the woods and relatively undeveloped.

rooms	8 twins/doubles.
price	80 YTL. Singles 60 YTL.
meals	20-30 YTL.
closed	December-February.
directions	34km from Kemer: use Olimpos exit, near Olimpos/Çavuş junction.
airport	95km from Antalya Airport.

	Refiye & Bülent Sağocak
tel	+90 (242) 8921133
email	olympus@daphneevi.com
web	www.daphneevi.com

Guest house

Map 5 Entry 128

Eskiyeni

Yazır (Olimpos), 07350 Kumluca, Antalya

The back side of the ruins of Olympus – the area called Olimpos proper, as opposed to Çıralı – is a vast forest of umbrella pines crossed by torrents that grow wild in winter. A curious subculture of tree houses grew here 20 years ago in response to the building ban. More recently, the tree houses have begun to settle and grow roots, acquiring decent roofing and fine interiors, while keeping up the pretence of being temporary shacks not subject to the building code. The result is, perhaps, a little Hollywoodish in its improvisation but often creative and certainly full of fun. Eskiyeni ('Old-new') manages to bring together four or five different building styles in a riverbank garden of two acres. It has buildings in timber and adobe, a windmill and a traditional wooden storage house all patched together in seemingly haphazard fashion. The interiors are more conventional. The atmosphere is friendly and laid-back and the beach is two kilometres off at the head of a beautiful walking trail.

rooms	12: 10 twins/doubles, 2 apartments for 4.
price	Half board 70 YTL. Apartments 105 YTL. Singles 50 YTL.
meals	Half board only.
closed	November-April.
directions	34km from Kemer: use Olimpos exit from highway, continue toward ruins at Çavuş junction.
airport	95km from Antalya Airport.

	Tahir Taluer
tel	+90 (242) 8921341
fax	+90 (242) 8921362
email	taluer@yahoo.com
web	www.eskiyeni.com.tr

Guest house

Map 5 Entry 129

Olympus Lodge
(PK 38), Çıralı, 07980 Kemer, Antalya

Olympus Lodge combines extraordinary beauty of setting with an effortless elegance of style to create the perfect spot for total rest. A riot of abundance, the garden hides secret passages, unexpected ponds, impenetrable thickets and sudden clearings with hammocks slung across the trees. Peacocks, including some unreal albinos, strut the meticulously clipped turf. The evening air carries wafts of jasmine and the scent of a special bush that only releases its perfume on summer nights. The setting: a magnificent beach of coarse sand before you, the 7,000-foot peak of Lycian Olympus, snow-capped until late May, in the background, the ruins of a Roman city in the forest within strolling distance. Twelve simply yet comfortably furnished cabins lie low in the vast property. Dinner is served in style under the eucalyptus trees; rabbits and geese arrive on cue to share the crumbs. Mr Şimşek directed an engineering firm in Berlin before choosing to settle in Olympus. He basks in the late-found happiness of recently-born twins and spends his free time building a village of stone and adobe in the hills.

rooms	13: 12 twins/doubles, 1 suite.
price	300–350 YTL. Suite 360 YTL. Singles from 250 YTL.
meals	From 60 YTL, with wine.
closed	Never.
directions	30km from Kemer: use Çıralı exit, turn right in the village, veer left at end of the road, (unmarked).
airport	93km from Antalya Airport.

	Ziya Şimşek
tel	+90 (242) 8257171
fax	+90 (242) 8257173
email	info@olymposlodge.com.tr
web	www.olymposlodge.com.tr

Hotel

Map 5 Entry 130

Arcadia

Çıralı, 07980 Kemer, Antalya

If Olympus is for the gods, there is Arcadia for the mortals. It may not offer nectar and ambrosia for the banqueting table, but is a most beautiful place. Its five big chalets lie among the orange and olive groves beside a spectacular beach, and the mountain backdrop will fit most people's notion of a heavenly kingdom. The host is a political Turk who was tossed to many unlikely corners of the globe before he found this private idyll. His garden is large enough so you can subsist for days without having to bump into anyone else. The pinewood cabins are reasonably comfortable, though without much striving for elegance. Dine on super-fresh fish on a decked and parasoled terrace, bask in a hammock, snorkel or swim. Mr Doğan is a soft-spoken man, and delightful company to have on excursions to the sights in the area. Up on the hill behind Çıralı is the perpetual fire of Chimaera. It burns in a natural vent in the ground; when put out, it re-ignites on its own. The ancient Lycians saw in it the breath of a dragon, and built temples around the site.

rooms	5 cabins.
price	Half board 180 YTL. Singles 150 YTL.
meals	Half board only.
closed	December-March.
directions	34km from Kemer: use Çıralı exit, turn right in the village; at far (northern) end of the beach.
airport	93km from Antalya Airport.

Ahmet Doğan

tel	+90 (242) 8257340
fax	+90 (242) 8257226
email	info@arcadiaholiday.com
web	www.arcadiaholiday.com

Guest house

Map 5 Entry 131

Azur Hotel

Çıralı, 07980 Kemer, Antalya

The extended Altıntaş family – brothers, aunts, nephews, grandmothers – and their German bride, Ilse, are the owners of this charming, friendly hotel that consists of plain but comfortable garden bungalows set in a quasi-tropical garden in Çıralı. The bungalows were thoroughly modernised a few years ago, and furnished with all the conveniences of a modern mid-class hotel. They are so deeply buried among orange, palm and pomegranate trees that we had a hard time taking photographs. Also hidden in the garden are a children's playground, coops full of unusual poultry and some free-roaming rabbits, making this the perfect place for families with children. The beach of Olympus, one of the most spectacular on the Mediterranean coast, lies within a 10-minute walk down a garden alley. A modest restaurant belonging to the family of the hosts is down by the beach.

rooms	8 triples.
price	140 YTL. Singles 100 YTL.
meals	30-45 YTL, with wine.
closed	Never.
directions	34km from Kemer: use Çıralı exit, turn left in village.
airport	94km from Antalya Airport.

	Ahmet & Ilse Altıntaş
tel	+90 (242) 8257072
fax	+90 (242) 8257076
email	azurhotel@superonline.com

Guest house

Map 5 Entry 132

Kibala Hotel

Çıralı, 07980 Kemer, Antalya

Emilie is half-French, half-American and the sweetest sort of person. Bülent is courtly and mild-mannered. At the foot of an astonishingly vertical rock, buried in jasmine and orange trees, their garden shows the signs of genuine, spontaneous love. The four wooden cabins are all that can be legally constructed in tightly-regulated Çıralı: they are a good size, set well apart from each other and have pots of geraniums on their doorsteps. Living rooms come with sofabeds, mini bars and kettles. Bülent and Emilie run a nice bar-restaurant on the premises; they cook and serve in person and go out of their way to make their guests happy: they deserve to be much better known. Çıralı has over 60 modest *pansiyons* buried in spectacularly lush sub-tropical vegetation below the 2,400-metre peak of the Lycian Olympus; this one is situated at the inland end of the village, a 10-minute walk from the beach. Summer breezes, spectacular valley views, a library of guide books – and bicycles to get you to the bay in extra-quick time.

rooms	4 cabins for 2-4.
price	Half board 120 YTL. Singles 90 YTL.
meals	Half board only.
closed	Never.
directions	32km from Kemer: use Çıralı exit, before village entrance.
airport	92km from Antalya Airport.

	Bülent & Emilie Coşkun
tel	+90 (242) 8257096
fax	+90 (242) 8257203
email	kibalahotel@yahoo.com
web	www.kibalahotel.com

Guest house

Map 5 Entry 133

Sundance Nature Village

Faselis Cad., Tekirova, 07980 Kemer, Antalya

Squeezed between the muscular peaks of the Beydağı Mountains and the sea lies the Bay of Phaselis, a magnificent sweep of sand and forest that somehow remains un-built. On one side of the bay is Phaselis, an archaeological site of poetical beauty. Sundance occupies the other side, a vast tract of partly swampy wilderness; we haven't seen Africa but surely it must be like this. The camp — more 'a lifestyle and a philosophy' than a resort — has achieved near-cult status for its devotees. It has little to show in terms of either service or style; cleanliness is obviously not a top priority, either. Instead, there are free-roaming horses, some exotic wildfowl, farm animals and a spirit of easy-going fraternity. The owners are two young men who have spent part of their lives in America while the philosophical Mrs Miller, formerly an engineer, is in charge of day-to-day affairs. The bungalows come with mosquito-screened windows and solar-heated showers, there is one adobe cabin with air conditioning, some stilt-houses à la Kadir's (Olympus) and vast amounts of tent space. The sea is unbelievable.

rooms	12 cabins.
price	70-100 YTL. Singles from 45 YTL.
meals	20-30 YTL.
closed	Never.
directions	14km from Kemer: first left in Tekirova.
airport	70km from Antalya Airport.

	Gülden Miller
tel	+90 (242) 8214165
email	sundance@sundancecamp.com
web	www.sundancecamp.com

Camp

Map 5 Entry 134

Berke Ranch

Akçasaz Mvk. 186, Çamyuva, 07990 Kemer, Antalya

A riding and holiday club set at the foot of the Taurus Mountains, Berke faces away from the sea and the great tourist-processing centres of Kemer's beaches. The focus of the scenery is the Twin Rocks, a spectacular pair of granite towers that seem geologically unrelated to the mountains around them. Behind them rise the mighty peaks of the Lycian Olympus. Endless gardens of orange trees cover the lowland, though they are being slowly gnawed at the edges by the greedy bunkers of the newly rich. Spread over the generous grounds of the ranch are a low-lying main building, several two-storey villas, a fancy 'honeymoon suite', two convivial restaurants (one out, one in), a large swimming pool and the horses' quarters. The style aspires to elegance in a scaled-down version of Antalya's highly professionalised holiday establishments. There are lots of horses, with riding instructors and excursion leaders fluent in many languages. They organise four-to-seven day riding tours into remote parts of this mountainous country.

rooms	27 + 2: 26 twins/doubles, 1 suite. 2 houses for 4.	
price	Half board 150 YTL. Suite 270 YTL. Singles 95 YTL. Houses 270 YTL.	
meals	Half board only.	
closed	November-March.	
directions	6km from Kemer: Çamyuva-3 exit, turn inland.	
airport	60km from Antalya Airport.	

	Ayberk Bozkurt
tel	+90 (242) 8180333
fax	+90 (242) 8180560
email	info@hotel-berkeranch.com
web	www.hotel-berkeranch.com

Hotel & Self-catering

Map 5 Entry 135

Tekeli Konakları

Dizdar Hasan Sok., Kaleiçi, 07100 Antalya

The lavishly reconstituted Ottoman pasha's residence is set on a bluff above the lively old harbour of Antalya. Eight dissimilar bedrooms, set round an enclosed courtyard off a quiet old street, are a feast of ancient and half-forgotten Turkish arts and crafts. There are miniature-painted ceilings in the Ottoman manner and handmade ceramics from Kütahya, natural-dye fabrics that have been woven under the supervision of Arts Institute professors and natural olive oil soaps made in hill villages. The superb woodwork is entirely made of cedar whose sweet scent alternates with the even sweeter wafts of bakery from the pastry shop below. The staff are efficiently professional and friendly, there's a pretty pool that is floodlit at night and the restaurant — inside or out — specialises in old-fashioned Turkish upper-crust cuisine. Overall, this is a rather luxurious hotel with a pristine-new feel and our only gripe would be the nightly noise from the popular entertainment venues around the corner.

rooms	8 twins/doubles.
price	200 YTL. Singles 175 YTL.
meals	45-60 YTL, with wine.
closed	Never.
directions	In Antalya: enter Old City at clock tower, follow street to end, then turn right.
airport	14km from Antalya Airport.

	Yakup Kayacı
tel	+90 (242) 2445465
fax	+90 (242) 2426714
email	mirya@superonline.com
web	www.tekeli.com.tr

Hotel

Ninova Pansiyon

Barbaros Mah.Hamit Efendi Sok. 9, Kaleiçi, 07100 Antalya

A quiet, friendly house on a pretty Kaleiçi street two blocks in from Hadrian's Gate, the building has been thoroughly renovated and furnished with moderation. It has a delightful garden stuffed with orange trees to which you can escape from the sun, and a cosy common room. But what draws us to this modest little place whenever we are in town is the hospitality of Ms Malhas, an Armenian lady from Istanbul who is everyone's friend and confidante and is an indispensable source of gossip about the comings and goings of Antalya. Like all Armenian ladies she cooks deliciously and she will even read your fortune in the dregs of a cup of Turkish coffee. The Old Town of Antalya retains its 2,200-year-old fortifications (hence the local name, Kaleiçi, which means In-the-Fort) and its 800 registered houses from the Ottoman era. Once reduced to dereliction, it was saved through an ambitious urban renewal programme launched in the 1980s. Impressive reminders of the city's Roman, Byzantine and Turkish pasts lie scattered in the narrow twisting alleys.

rooms	15 twins/doubles.
price	70 YTL. Singles 52 YTL.
meals	30 YTL.
closed	Never.
directions	In Antalya Old Town: two blocks in from Hadrian's Gate.
airport	14km from Antalya Airport.

Hripsime Malhas

tel	+90 (242) 2486114
fax	+90 (242) 2489684
email	info@ninovapension.com

Guest house

Map 5 / City Map p30   Entry 137

Tuvana Hotel

Tuzcular Mah. Karanlık Sok. 18, Kaleiçi, 07100 Antalya

In a quiet jasmine-scented back street in Old Antalya you will find this well-appointed small hotel, which has grown in leaps and bounds to become one of the most highly-regarded places to stay in hotel-infested Old Antalya. Credit goes to the young owner-manager team, Mr Tankut and Ms Sümer, who believe in being ever-present and hands-on – an exception in a town where the norm is absentee owners and fast-circulating managers. The main house is actually the home of Mr Tankut's grandmother (her brass bridal bed still graces one of the rooms). Other historic houses along the alley joined the hotel in 1999, 2001 and 2004, each displaying greater sophistication, larger and more expensive rooms and finer accessories than the earlier – a mark of increasing professionalism and a rising customer profile. The interiors are richly furnished in quasi-antiques. The walled courtyard with full-scale swimming pool, well-stocked bar and shady orange grove is a good place to spend summer days in blissful idleness.

rooms	34: 32 twins/doubles, 2 suites.
price	180–230 YTL. Suites 270 YTL. Singles from 140 YTL.
meals	30–45 YTL, with wine.
closed	Never.
directions	In Antalya Old Town: near Paşa Mosque.
airport	14km from Antalya Airport.

	Aziz Tankut & Nermin Sümer
tel	+90 (242) 2444054
fax	+90 (242) 2411981
email	info@tuvanahotel.com
web	www.tuvanahotel.com

Hotel

Atelya Pansiyon

Civelek Sok. 21, Kaleiçi, 07100 Antalya

The modest exterior of this restored old Antalya house does not prepare you for the charming patio that lies inside. The doors open into a cool alcove furnished in traditional style and a peaceful, leafy courtyard that is filled with the sweet scent of jasmine and the gurgle of an old fountain: there could be no better retreat to withdraw to at the end of a hot day. The *pansiyon* is actually three houses clustered around an old Antalya alley. The main house is the real old-timer: the traditional timber-and-plaster construction is well suited to the climate, being light and breezy rather than oppressive and dull like its modern rival, concrete. The third house has larger rooms decorated in a sultans-and-pashas style that strikes us as being a bit sugary – but wait until you see the penthouse, as inviting and comfortable a living space as there is in all Antalya. Mr Kaçaroğlu runs his characterful hotel in a sensitive and refined manner.

rooms	30: 28 twins/doubles, 2 suites.
price	60 YTL. Suites 100 YTL. Singles from 50 YTL.
meals	30-45 YTL, with wine.
closed	Never.
directions	In Antalya: in Old Town four blocks in from Hadrian's Gate.
airport	14km from Antalya Airport.

	Hakan Kaçaroğlu
tel	+90 (242) 2416416
fax	+90 (242) 2412848
email	atelyahotel1@hotmail.com
web	www.atelyahotel.com

Hotel

Map 5/City Map p30 Entry 139

Minyon Town House
Tabakhane Sok. 31, Kaleiçi, 07100 Antalya

There are charming hotels galore in the alleys of Old Antalya but finding one that is furnished and managed in good taste is harder than it might at first appear. So it was a pleasure to discover this very dainty and utterly feminine house stationed on the quietest of the old town's quiet little squares. It has a wonderfully cosy interior, which is as spit-and-polish and as neat as it gets, and a delightful small garden with a bijou pool stylishly decked and uncontaminated by plastic. The furniture is unexaggeratedly elegant and the pebble mosaic of the lobby floor is nothing short of a masterpiece. Mrs Feray, an elegant lady from Istanbul who stumbled into hotel-keeping by happy accident, lives next door in the same garden and enjoys inviting her guests over for coffee on her own private patio. The scent of orange blossoms is overwhelming in spring. Above all, there's a private beach, a ten-minute walk away at the bottom of Antalya's *falaise*. All other things being equal, it is worth going there just for the sake of the five-o'clock cookies.

rooms	9: 8 twins/doubles, 1 suite.
price	180 YTL. Suite 210 YTL. Singles from 140 YTL.
meals	Restaurants nearby.
closed	Never.
directions	In Antalya: third street left after Kesik Minare Mosque.
airport	14km from Antalya Airport.

	Ernan Feray
tel	+90 (242) 2471147
fax	+90 (242) 2478481
email	info@minyonhotel.com
web	www.minyonhotel.com

Hotel

Bagana Horse Club

Yukarı Karaman, 07310 Düzlerçamı, Antalya

Bagana is a riding club hotel set in a beautiful fold of the Taurus mountains. The host is a German woman of great charm who combines a German passion for detail with the friendly ease of her adopted country. The mix produces all the mod cons and services of a country club without departing too far from the rural feel. The cottages are simply but comfortably fitted and set unobtrusively in an orange grove; there's an indoor/outdoor restaurant that overlooks the stables, a tennis court, a sauna and a lively pool. Nights are wonderfully quiet under the bright highland sky. The centrepiece of the property is the riding school and the horses are sprightly and well-trained. The terrain is an explorer's dream, full of beautiful and little travelled paths and enough interesting destinations to fill two weeks' worth of hiking and horseback touring. High points include the ruins of ancient Termessos, set above a terrifying ravine, and the high pastures of the Döşemealtı region where vast flocks of sheep roam in summer.

rooms	8 twins/doubles.
price	70 YTL. Singles 55 YTL.
meals	20-30 YTL.
closed	Never.
directions	17km from Antalya: Korkuteli road, marked right at km7 marker.
airport	25km from Antalya Airport.

	Susanne Pape
tel	+90 (242) 4252270
fax	+90 (242) 4252055
email	info@baganahorseclub.com
web	www.baganahorseclub.com

Hotel

Map 5 Entry 141

Gönülköşküm Highland House

Bayatbademleri, 07800 Korkuteli, Antalya

Long ago, when swimming in the sea was not a fashionable pastime and only workmen flaunted their tan, the people of southern Turkey would migrate to the mountains each year to escape the summer heat. Even now, older-style people look with pity on the crowds who bake on Antalya's beaches in July. At a *yayla* like Bayatbademleri you may need a sweater when Antalya is a sticky furnace below. Mr and Mrs Çoban, both engineers, have built their dream home amid the arid rocks of the high Taurus: Gönülköşküm ('My Heart's Lodge') is an attempt to bring the *yayla* culture to the modern age. The village must once have been a primordial sort of place; now it is mangled by the *beton* villas of the newly rich. But the hotel stands out of their sight at the outer edge of the village. The sheer labour of keeping a good garden in such a harsh setting deserves congratulations; so does the breakfast, full of local goodies and Turkish home classics. The bungalow-style rooms are outfitted unexcitingly in a simple modern manner. Mountain bikes are provided for roaming around the pine-clad hills.

rooms	11: 9 twins/doubles, 2 singles.
price	85 YTL. Singles 60 YTL.
meals	25 YTL.
closed	Never.
directions	32km from Antalya: Korkuteli road, right (marked) at km 25 to Bayatbademler.
airport	40km from Antalya Airport.

	Ümran Kantarcı
tel	+90 (242) 6691235
fax	+90 (242) 6691236
email	info@gonulkoskum.com
web	www.gonulkoskum.com

Guest house

Map 5 Entry 142

Kanyon Lodge
Karabük, 07600 Manavgat, Antalya

Turn inland along the Köprüçay river towards Beşkonak and you soon leave modern Turkey behind. The road first runs through rolling farmland then enters a mighty gorge cutting through the Taurus Mountains. About 45km on, perched dizzyingly high over the canyon, is the Roman bridge that lends the river its Turkish name (*köprü* means bridge). Further up, hidden in a primitive village at more than 1,000 metres, lie the Roman ruins of Selge. For many years Hüsnü Tuğ's Kanyon Restaurant & Trout Farm was the only inhabited stop of any sort along this virgin route; now there are nearly a dozen trout-and-kebab stations on the way. Hüsnü has meanwhile added a number of solidly-built stone-and-timber rooms to his establishment. The rooms are clean, pine-clad and comfortable with white shower rooms and heating for the cooler months. There's a good-sized swimming pool with plastic loungers and, with the river rushing past the garden and impenetrable forest rising in the background, the setting is idyllic. A good place to get away from the hectic commercialism of the Antalya coast.

rooms	24: 16 twins/doubles, 8 cabins for 4.
price	Half board 70 YTL. Cabins 70 YTL. Singles 45 YTL.
meals	Half board only.
closed	Never.
directions	67km from Manavgat: Antalya road, right toward Beşkonak and Selge.
airport	120km from Antalya Airport.

	Hüsnü Tuğ
tel	+90 (242) 7653201
fax	+90 (242) 7653202
email	info@kanyonlodge.com
web	www.kanyonlodge.com

Hotel

Map 5 Entry 143

Villa Lapin

Şelale Mah., 07600 Manavgat, Antalya

A mere 10-minute drive from the touristy razzmatazz of Side, Manavgat inhabits a different world. The town's pride and joy are the Manavgat Falls – not quite a Niagara perhaps, but a lovely sight nevertheless. In the local teashop you can actually strike up a conversation without anyone trying to sell you T-shirts or rugs, while the ruins of several Roman cities lie all but forgotten in the mountains above. Lapin Pension occupies a huge and leafy garden on the banks of the Manavgat River, a short distance below the falls. Your hosts are young Hasan and his German sweetheart. They recently returned from Germany to take over the family *pansiyon* and together they offer an immense amount of beginner's goodwill and seem determined to make it a very good hotel indeed. Bedrooms are traditional-simple, there are two lovely terraces for meals (grilled meats and fish, market-fresh vegetables) and some cosy lounges – but it is the soothing combination of river and garden that makes this place really special.

rooms	6: 5 twins/doubles, 1 triple.
price	90 YTL. Singles 80 YTL.
meals	20-30 YTL.
closed	November-February.
directions	2km from Manavgat: on the left bank of the river 2km up (eastwards) from centre; hard to find.
airport	70km from Antalya Airport.

	Kira & Hasan Öz
tel	+90 (242) 7429146
fax	+90 (242) 7429146
email	kira_hasan@hotmail.com
web	www.villa-lapin.com

Guest house

Map 5 Entry 144

Taşkonak

Acinar Mvk. 13, Karakocalı, 07400 Alanya, Antalya

An impressive neo-Turkish chateau in the hills behind Alanya, surrounded by miles of citrus grove and farmland in the earliest stages of succumbing to real estate. The beach is five kilometres away and the mighty fortress of Alanya is a blip on the horizon. The hotel has a private, somewhat clubbish atmosphere. It started out as a private folly of Mr Saz, a carpet merchant, and primarily hosts his circle of guests from Austria, although outsiders are just as welcome. The initial effect is grandiose: a grand stairway of the rarest red marble, a colonnade of carved sandstone pillars, a king-size swimming pool and interior spaces designed to impress. Bedrooms come in different sizes, the best with balconies, and are comfortable and correct though a touch impersonal; a domed, traditional Turkish bath promises steamy pleasure and the garden is meticulously groomed and full of unusual species. Mrs Saz presides over the show in person and cultivates an informal 'country house' style: dinner is often served at the common table and guests often feel free to get behind the bar.

rooms	16 twins/doubles.
price	Full board 190-230 YTL. Singles from 110 YTL.
meals	Full board only.
closed	November-April.
directions	5km from Alanya: from the outer peripheral road, toward Oba, signed for Karakocalı.
airport	130km from Antalya Airport.

	Selma Saz
tel	+90 (242) 5388688
fax	+90 (242) 5388687
email	info@taskonakhotel.com
web	www.taskonakhotel.com

Hotel

Map 5 Entry 145

Bedesten Club Hotel

İç Kale, 07400 Alanya, Antalya

A rare alternative to the relentless concrete uniformity of Alanya's hotels. The setting is a renovated *bedesten* – a merchants' inn and warehouse – in the historic citadel of Alanya, soaring 200 vertiginous metres above the sea. The neighbourhood is straight from an engraving of the Old Orient, complete with a handsome Ottoman mosque, the ivy-covered ruins of an old *kervansaray* and scattered tombstones in the shade of tall cypresses and gnarled fig trees. The stupendous cistern in the backyard is probably Byzantine, if not older. The main building is a rectangular cloister with 30 rather small and spartan rooms set around it, all thick stone walls and small windows. More pleasant are the two deluxe suites in the newer wing. There isn't a great deal in the way of style here, but the staff are friendly in a pleasantly unhurried, Mediterranean way, the generous gardens offer plenty of scope for a quiet holiday. The view from the terrace alone is worth the visit.

rooms	32: 30 twins/doubles, 2 suites.
price	100 YTL. Suites 160 YTL. Singles from 80 YTL.
meals	30-45 YTL, with wine.
closed	November-April.
directions	2km from Alanya harbour: in the citadel.
airport	128km from Antalya Airport.

	Hakan Derin
tel	+90 (242) 5121234
fax	+90 (242) 5137934
email	info@bedestenhotel.com
web	www.bedestenhotel.com

Hotel

Map 5 Entry 146

Photo Turkish Culture & Tourism Office

cappadocia

cappadocia: cave hotels

The fantastic landscape of Cappadocia is shaped out of volcanic ash, eroded over the ages into strange formations known as 'fairy chimneys', then dug by human hand into cave homes, cellars, monks' cells, entire villages, several hundred gnome-sized churches and more than 20 underground towns. The carving still goes on: some of the most outstanding small hotels featured in this section are actually caves cut into Cappadocia's volcanic rock.

The hub of the region is a 15km x 15km triangle defined by the towns of Nevesehir, Avanos and Urgup.

- Urgup is the obvious base for most visitors - compact, striking and well-furnished with tourist resources.

- Göreme is younger and cheaper, while fantastically shaped Uchisar is the least lively of the three.

- Beyond lie some little-known gems - Mustafapaşa (formally Sinasos) with its fascinating old Greek architecture, Ayvalı with its unspoilt village charm, and Guzelyurt, with its imposing former theological school.

Karballa Hotel

68500 Güzelyurt, Aksaray

Güzelyurt is one of Cappadocia's many undiscovered gems. The town faces the perfect cone of the Hasandağ volcano. It has an old quarter that simply breathes character, quaintness and charm, and a valley of rock monasteries that is as good as any in Cappadocia, yet remains virtually untouched by tourism. St Gregory Nazianzen, a 4th-century Father of the Church, spent part of his life in this town, which was then called Karballa or Karvali. His relics were transferred to Greece from the local church – now a mosque – in 1924. Hotel Karballa occupies the 19th-century buildings of a former Greek Orthodox theological seminary. Kirkit Tourism, a pioneer of youth and activity tourism around Turkey, operates the hotel in a spirit of friendly indolence and the facilities are somewhat dorm-style, as befits the monastic spirit of the place. The area offers some of the best hiking and horseback riding in all Cappadocia – notably the Ihlara Valley, a splendid canyon that richly rewards the six-hour trek along its full length.

rooms	20: 8 twins/doubles, 12 family rooms for 4.
price	Half board 85 YTL. Family rooms 150 YTL. Singles from 55 YTL.
meals	20-30 YTL.
closed	15 November-March.
directions	66km from Nevşehir: on the way to Ihlara via Derinkuyu.
airport	160km from Kayseri Airport.

	Osman Diler
tel	+90 (382) 4512103
fax	+90 (382) 4512107
email	kirkit@gediknet.com

Hotel

Map 3 & 6 Entry 147

Museum Hotel

Tekelli Mah. 1., 50240 Uçhisar, Nevşehir

A cosy and colourful hotel that is both a deeply comfortable place to spend the night and a cultural treat – hence the name. Mr Tosun has furnished his hotel with a splendid collection of Anatolian antiques and handicrafts, including some of the finest Turkish carpets we have ever seen displayed in a place to stay. The overall effect is a bit Aladdin's-lampish, but good taste and goodwill are nonetheless evident at every turn. We especially liked the old-fashioned satin-covered quilts – a Turkish touch which you won't find in any of today's modern-minded hotels. Half the rooms are built of masonry while the others constitute a labyrinth of beautifully intimate, refurbished caves cut into one side of Uçhisar's great rock. The caves are posh: don't be surprised to find several jacuzzi baths deep in the bowels of the earth here. Mr Tosun runs a travel agency as well as a network of internet-based travel services, so this is an ideal base to start from when planning your activities in the region of Cappadocia. A gleaming new pool awaits you at the end of your active day.

rooms	21: 5 twins/doubles, 16 suites.
price	135 YTL. Suites 200-650 YTL. Singles from 100 YTL.
meals	30-45 YTL, with wine.
closed	Never.
directions	In Uçhisar: Göreme road, up on narrow road at sales stands below Uçhisar fort.
airport	77km from Kayseri Airport.

	Ömer Tosun
tel	+90 (384) 2192220
fax	+90 (384) 2192444
email	info@museum-hotel.com
web	www.museum-hotel.com

Hotel

Map 3 & 6 Entry 148

Les Maisons de Cappadoce

Semiramis AŞ, Belediye Meydanı 6, 50240 Uçhisar, Nevşehir

Uçhisar is the most striking of Cappadocian villages, a stone-age rabbit warren at the foot of the region's tallest fairy chimney. Here, a French architect fell in love with the millennial rhythms of Anatolia, acquired a string of cave dwellings, previously deserted by the upwardly-mobile villagers, and converted them with aesthetic élan into contemporary two-storey houses. He lets them by the day as fully-equipped holiday homes. Mr Avizou is a man of very Gallic temperament – charming and difficult. His houses and studios combine extraordinary simplicity of concept with an unfailing sense of detail and harmonious colours. One house has a dream-like garden; another has a vast underground cellar; several have exceptional views; all are enticing. There are fairy chimneys outside and nooks of indescribable charm and surprising topography everywhere. Services are limited, though breakfast is delivered daily as a basket. Other than that you are pretty much on your own to enjoy, for a few days, the private cave home of your dreams.

rooms	12 houses/studios: 4 for 2, 3 for 4, 5 for 6.
price	140 YTL. Houses for 4, 210 YTL. Houses for 6, 360 YTL.
meals	Meals by arrangement.
closed	November–April.
directions	In Uçhisar: office/reception on main square.
airport	77km from Kayseri Airport.

	Jacques Avizou
tel	+90 (384) 2192813
fax	+90 (384) 2192782
email	info@cappadoce.com
web	www.cappadoce.com

Self-catering

Map 3 & 6 Entry 149

Gamirasu Cave Hotel

Ayvalı (Aravan), 50360 Ürgüp, Nevşehir

Ayvalı (also called Aravan) is a small Cappadocian town barely touched by the tourist hullabaloo of places like Ürgüp and Göreme. A fantastic gorge of ancient rock dwellings – some still inhabited – cuts across the town, unseen until you stumble over it by chance. There are a couple of guest houses here but no-one as yet who tries to sell you carpets or gewgaws, yet the main tourist attractions are a 15-minute drive away. Gamirasu occupies a stone *konak* and the neighbouring patchwork of rock cells built deep into the side of the gorge; it all blends smoothly into the otherworldly landscape and it is fitting that some rooms were apparently used as monks' cells in the past. The hotel started out in 1999 with a German owner and a spiritual-holistic bent, although more traditional Turkish hospitality has since taken over. The heart of the establishment is Mr Baştutan, a local man of personal charisma and an easy smile. His visitors' book gushes with praise from guests from the four corners of the world.

rooms	18: 13 twins/doubles, 5 suites.
price	95-140 YTL. Suites 240 YTL. Singles from 70 YTL.
meals	20-30 YTL.
closed	Never.
directions	11km from Ürgüp: Mustafapaşa-Kaymaklı road to Ayvali; bottom of the gully (driveable).
airport	75km from Kayseri Airport.

	İbrahim Baştutan, Süleyman Çakır
tel	+90 (384) 3415825
fax	+90 (384) 3417487
email	info@gamirasu.com
web	www.gamirasu.com

Hotel

Map 3 & 6 Entry 150

Gül Konakları

Sümer Sok., Mustafapaşa (Sinasos), 50420 Ürgüp, Nevşehir

Mustafapaşa is architecturally the most interesting of Cappadocian towns and this is an Ottoman dream-palace re-created in lavish style in a pair of the town's finest historic houses. All the details of a proper pasha's residence are here. You have a glazed *köşk* – a garden pavilion – where you can take your coffee and recline on the round-about divans. There is a Turkish *hamam* complete with scrub-wielding professional attendants. There is even a rose garden in the best Ottoman tradition: the name of the hotel means Rose Mansions. Other details, such as the fine collection of 19th-century engravings and the mirror lounge with fireplace, suggest a more European touch – a pasha who went to school in England perhaps? Some bedrooms have arched ceilings, most have small windows and the living rooms are on a scale that one associates with much larger hotels. Combined with the small number of private rooms this gives the place a somewhat formal feel and the staff's well-groomed professionalism adds to the atmosphere of efficient impersonality.

rooms	19: 15 twins/doubles, 4 suites.
price	Half board 210 YTL. Singles 160 YTL.
meals	Half board only.
closed	Never.
directions	5km from Ürgüp: south to Mustafapaşa, right at town entrance.
airport	70km from Kayseri Airport.

	Yakup & Mustafa Dinler, Yusuf Örnek
tel	+90 (384) 3535486
fax	+90 (384) 3535487
email	info@rosemansions.com
web	www.rosemansions.com

Hotel

Map 3 & 6 Entry 151

Club Natura Cappadocia

Sümer Sok. 16 , Mustafapaşa (Sinasos), 50420 Ürgüp, Nevşehir

A beautiful old Greek mansion in Mustafapaşa/Sinasos, a Cappadocian town remarkable for just that: so many elegant old houses abandoned to gentle decline since the ethnic exchange of the 1920s. The house remains un-renovated and under-maintained, full of creaky charm and huge under-used spaces which would be the first to be rationalised away when the modernisers go to work. The ground-floor rooms are vaulted in stone; the state rooms on the upper floor have high, finely patterned ceilings and some of their wall paintings intact – although you have to go downstairs for the loo. There are also some 'newer' (50- or 60-year-old) rooms in the annexe. Otherwise there are few comforts to speak of and fewer services, but for sheer historic film-set atmosphere this is hard to beat. Club Natura is a German outfit that offers cultural experience tours in little-known and out-of-the way parts of the world. Their groups are sometimes here but otherwise the house is open to all comers. Do take home some of the cellar-stored grape syrups and apricot jams.

rooms	9 twins/doubles, some with own bath or shower.
price	85 YTL. Singles 45 YTL.
meals	Meals by arrangement.
closed	November-April.
directions	5km from Ürgüp: south to Mustafapaşa, right at town entrance.
airport	100km from Kayseri Airport.

	Aysel Koch
tel	+90 (384) 3535030
fax	+90 (384) 3535430
email	info@clubnatura.com
web	www.clubnatura.com

Guest house

Map 3 & 6 Entry 152

Lamia

Mustafapaşa (Sinasos), 50420 Ürgüp, Nevşehir

A charming lady of part-German background is the owner, decorator, host and namesake of this highly personal little guest house hidden from view in the quiet back streets of Mustafapaşa, formerly the Greek-populated Sinasos. She is an accomplished artist who left her native Istanbul to settle in Cappadocia. She lives here with her three lively dalmatians, cooks in central European style and serves opulent breakfasts. The guest house is a stone house with arched chambers in old Cappadocian style surrounding a courtyard filled with flowers and a basking cat. The rooms – and bathrooms – are decorated with a surfeit of precious objects, antique furnishings, embroideries, old photographs and Lamia's own paintings. Breakfast is served, weather permitting, on the flat roof with a view over the town. A stroll in the cobblestoned lanes reveals many wonderful old mansions in various stages of decay, hidden cave-churches and an impressive Turkish *kervansaray* (hostelry) which now houses carpet workshops.

rooms	5 twins/doubles.
price	95 YTL. Singles 54 YTL.
meals	Meals by arrangement.
closed	November-March.
directions	5km from Ürgüp: south to Mustafapaşa, right then left in town.
airport	70km from Kayseri Airport.

	Lamia Arslan
tel	+90 (384) 3535413
fax	+90 (384) 3535044

Guest house

Map 3 & 6 Entry 153

Fairy Chimney Inn

Güvercinlik Sok. 3/7, 50180 Göreme, Nevşehir

The paradox is that you should have to be German, and a doctor of anthropology, too, to build so completely authentic a Cappadocian house. The locals prefer cement; the urbanites worry too much about design; the true primitive is hard to capture. Andus wrote his dissertation on the cave houses of Göreme; then he found the woman of his dreams in one and decided to become part of the landscape himself. He has taken forever to carve out his cave. We have waited five years and hope it will be just about ready by 2005 – *inşallah*. As it stands, it is a stunning labyrinth. Best of all, it makes no perceptible effort to fit the rock into a pre-conceived plan. If a room is thimble-sized, it is made into a comfortable thimble. A window may be below floor level but there is always enough light. A wonderful Turkish bath is fitted into an old wine press. The atmosphere is easy-going and un-authoritarian, bordering on the bohemian; the setting is a dream-like valley, uncontaminated by the hustle of touristy Göreme 10 minutes below.

rooms	8: 7 twins/doubles, 1 suite, some with own bath or shower.
price	80 YTL. Suite 95 YTL. Singles 45 YTL.
meals	Meals by arrangement.
closed	Never.
directions	In Göreme: in the old upper section.
airport	68km from Kayseri Airport.

	Gülcan & Andus Emge
tel	+90 (384) 2712655
fax	+90 (384) 2712862
email	contact@fairychimney.com
web	www.fairychimney.com

Hotel

Map 3 & 6 Entry 154

Kelebek Hotels

Aydınlı Mah. 22, 50180 Göreme, Nevşehir

A fairy chimney looks as unreal as it sounds. It is a tall cone-shaped rock, often with a hat on top, having a voluptuously curvy shape and the skin of an elephant. Göreme is full of fairy chimneys. Two of the nicest sort, about eight metres tall, stand in the courtyard of Kelebek Pension. They have rooms cut inside them, basic if cosy; when Ali – no Baba – tried to modernise them by adding a loo, he got into trouble with the preservation authorities. Now his establishment consists of two parts. The old *pansiyon* has the fairy chimneys and a long pedigree as former backpackers' haven, although it has been thoroughly upgraded in recent years – apart from the still unplumbed fairy rooms noted above. The new part is a splendidly reconstructed 'boutique hotel' standing in a large garden on the edge of the town, two streets away. The rooms in this part are stylishly done in the latest Cappadocian fashion – hand-carved doors and jacuzzis, antique kilims and suites with sitting areas, some suitable for families. The view over the Cappadocian moonscape is fantastic.

rooms	21: 11 twins/doubles, 10 suites.
price	54-90 YTL. Suites 140 YTL. Singles from 35 YTL.
meals	10-20 YTL.
closed	Never.
directions	In Göreme.
airport	75km from Kayseri Airport.

	Ali Yavuz
tel	+90 (384) 2712531
fax	+90 (384) 2712763
email	ali@kelebekhotel.com
web	www.kelebekhotel.com

Hotel

Map 3 & 6 Entry 155

Razziya Evi

Yeni Cami Mah. Cingilli Sok. 24, 50400 Ürgüp, Nevşehir

Ürgüp abounds in elegant cave hotels as well as cheap backpackers' and carpetmen's joints. But the choices are not too many if you look for a place in between – one that is modest, pleasant, friendly and un-sleazy, as well as inexpensive. Razziya House fits that description and it's hard to think of any others that do. Queen Razzia, who ruled in Delhi in the 13th century, was the first and probably only woman to reign in her own right in an Islamic land (she was, naturally, beheaded in the end). Romy, who chose the name, is a soft-spoken French-Swiss woman who does not strike one as someone with regal ambitions. Bedrooms are divided between those in a charming 400-year-old Greek house and a second, younger building, and have been decorated in an attractive and understated manner: soft fabrics against soft stone, good rugs and wrought-iron beds. The garden is well-shaded and pleasant and instead of a jacuzzi there is a lovely *hamam* built into the bowels of the Cappadocian rock.

rooms	7: 6 twins/doubles, 1 suite for 4.
price	65 YTL. Suite 100 YTL. Singles from 40 YTL.
meals	Meals by arrangement.
closed	Never.
directions	In Ürgüp: behind New Mosque.
airport	65km from Kayseri Airport.

Orhan & Romy Çelik
tel	+90 (384) 3415089
fax	+90 (384) 3412370
email	razziya@hotmail.com
web	www.razziyaevi.com

Guest house

Map 3 & 6 Entry 156

Room with a View

Esbelli Mah. 40, 50400 Ürgüp, Nevşehir

This must be the ultimate in cave luxury: a wholly private suite, furnished opulently and in somewhat American style, tucked away discreetly in the stone-age warren of Ürgüp's old cave district. And if you feel funny about spending your holiday in a cave, consider this: where else in Turkey do you get a 100-square-metre bedroom with a panoramic window over the entire town? The suite is attached to the home-cave of Mr and Mrs Yüksel, who succumbed to the lure of Cappadocia and moved here from the big city. He is a jazz fan who will share his enthusiasm with his guests; she is a painter and crafstwoman who also runs a giftshop of her own highly original handiwork in downtown Ürgüp. Fluent in English, they offer an elegant and comfortable environment – and superb breakfast – to their guests.

rooms	1 suite.
price	260 YTL.
meals	Restaurants nearby.
closed	Never.
directions	In Ürgüp: Nevşehir exit, right at Club Ürgüp/Turasan Winery.
airport	65km from Kayseri Airport.

Selim & Nuray Yüksel

tel	+90 (384) 3414967
fax	+90 (384) 3416257
email	sevim@argonautturkey.com

Guest house

Map 3 & 6 Entry 157

Kayadam

Esbelli Mah. 6, 50400 Ürgüp, Nevşehir

The cave-chapel next door goes back to the 9th century and some rooms may even have been used as burial chambers in Roman times. For the next millennium or two they served as comfortable dwellings. Now they are reborn as a small hotel of great charm. But the most memorable aspect of Kayadam (which simply means 'Rock House') is unquestionably the hostess. Mrs Çiner is a most graceful lady from Istanbul who, along with her son, a French-educated engineering professor, fell for the lure of cave-living. She first moved into a Cappadocian cave 15 years ago and received so many guests that she finally decided to run a proper hotel. Her main house has six modest but comfortably fitted rooms, furnished with country fabrics and the odd polished antique and re-carved to take bathrooms and other modern essentials. A second house a short walk up the hill is a self-contained family unit refurbished with greater panache than the main house. Mrs Çiner serves a delightful breakfast and the view over the Cappadocian landscape is nothing short of breathtaking.

rooms	8: 7 twins/doubles, 1 family room.
price	120 YTL. Family room 200 YTL. Singles from 80 YTL.
meals	Meals by arrangement.
closed	November–March.
directions	In Ürgüp: Nevşehir exit, right at Club Ürgüp/Turasan Winery (poorly marked).
airport	65km from Kayseri Airport.

	Kısmet Çiner
tel	+90 (384) 3416623
fax	+90 (384) 3415982
email	kayadam@kayadam.com
web	www.kayadam.com

Guest house

Map 3 & 6 Entry 158

Elkep Evi Cave House

Esbelli Mah. 26, 50400 Ürgüp, Nevşehir

An excellent cave hotel in Ürgüp's Cavern Hill that offers, like its neighbours, a fabulous atmosphere and exotic setting. The bonus here is larger and airier rooms, serene in their Turkish rusticity, each with a private terrace carved into a nook of the cliff and a gorgeous view over the Cappadocian dreamscape. The wealth of architectural detail and invention draws you in and you end up falling quite in love with this infinitely malleable stone womb. Breakfast in the hilltop garden on kilim-clad seats includes the delicious homemade savoury pastries known as *gozleme*. Haydar, an energetic host, presides over the house with his strong personal presence. Elkep Evi was formerly called Agartha Cave House. The Agarthans reportedly withdrew to a network of subterranean cities – enclosed ecosystems beneath the earth's crust – around the time when mankind invaded the surface of the globe with destructive drive. They submit, we are told, to the government of the Inner World and act as custodians of the sacred records and teachings of various ancient and perished cultures.

rooms	21: 19 twins/doubles, 2 suites .
price	100 YTL. Suites 170 YTL. Singles from 80 YTL.
meals	Meals by arrangement.
closed	Never.
directions	In Ürgüp: up toward Nevşehir exit, right at Club Ürgüp/Turasan Winery.
airport	65km from Kayseri Airport.

	Haydar Haykır, Leslie Harakawa
tel	+90 (384) 3416000
fax	+90 (384) 3418089
email	info@elkepevi.com
web	www.elkepevi.com

Hotel

Map 3 & 6 Entry 159

Esbelli Evi
Esbelli Sok. 8, 50400 Ürgüp, Nevşehir

A Cappadocian classic, much imitated but never quite equalled in its measured attention to detail and its understated perfectionism. There may be posher rivals, but Esbelli remains the world's classiest cave. Süha Ersöz, a lawyer and a fastidious bachelor, treats customers as his personal guests; only a tiny name plate gives any outward sign of his hotel. A rich CD collection (Bach, Couperin, some jazz) stands at guests' disposal in the common room, as does a refrigerator in the kitchen, well-stocked with liquor. The guestbook gushes with praise from Ankara's diplomatic community – a dozen ambassadors have written their names there, in company with some illustrious guests. Behind the façade of a splendid old stone mansion lies a labyrinth of hidden courtyards, stone stairways and nine rooms carved into Cappadocia's soft volcanic rock. The Honeymoon Room, with antique brass bedstead, occupies a real fairy chimney. The name of the house refers to the section of old Ürgüp where most dwellings are cut into the cliff. There is a striking view from here with half of Cappadocia under your feet.

rooms	9: 8 twins/doubles, 1 suite.
price	130 YTL. Suite 200 YTL. Singles from 90 YTL.
meals	Restaurants nearby.
closed	15 November-February.
directions	In Ürgüp: up toward Nevşehir exit, right at Club Ürgüp/Turasan Winery (poorly marked).
airport	65km from Kayseri Airport.

	Süha Ersöz
tel	+90 (384) 3413395
fax	+90 (384) 3418848
email	suha@esbelli.com.tr
web	www.esbelli.com.tr

Hotel

Map 3 & 6 Entry 160

Yunak Evleri

Yunak Mah., 50400 Ürgüp, Nevşehir

Mr Görürgöz made a fortune as the founder of a fashionable Istanbul restaurant, then invested in a cluster of utterly archaic cave dwellings cut into a cliff in Ürgüp. His audacious idea was to convert an entire cave neighbourhood into a single luxury hotel without so much as touching the outward appearance. So from the outside the houses look just as they have for the last 100 or even 1,000 years: an ancient warren of holes cut with seeming randomness into the dusty cliff; even the soot from old stoves remains. Inside, the spaces rival the best of the many-starred hotels of Turkey in style and comfort, charmingly embellished with antiques. Some rooms are set discreetly in their own courtyard, so you need never know who is staying next door. All are full of nooks and crannies, secret passageways and tiny terraces of the sort that normally occur in fairy tales. With a well-trained staff, the Yunak Houses offer a level of service seldom found in other small hotels in Cappadocia. And you can mountain-bike through the lunar landscape or go hot-air ballooning at dawn.

rooms	27: 23 twins/doubles, 4 suites.
price	160-180 YTL. Suites 240 YTL. Singles from 125 YTL.
meals	30-45 YTL, with wine.
closed	Never.
directions	In Ürgüp: up toward Nevşehir sign; hotel signed on right after Öğretmenevi (Teachers Club).
airport	65km from Kayseri Airport.

	Yusuf Görürgöz
tel	+90 (384) 3416920
fax	+90 (384) 3416924
email	yunak@yunak.com
web	www.yunak.com

Hotel

Map 3 & 6 Entry 161

Ürgüp Evi
Esbelli Mah., 50400 Ürgüp, Nevşehir

The cave dwellings of Cappadocia are not just fascinating exotica: furnished to modern standards, they also make delightful homes. Many outsiders – city Turks as well as foreigners – have made that discovery in recent years and the Cappadocian cave property market is booming. Faruk Maden, a stone-master who chipped out a few of the most brilliant cave conversions in Ürgüp, has reserved his crowning achievement for his own hotel, which he runs in person with open-hearted hospitality. This is an 11-room cave compound – including one extremely fancy new suite – surrounding a sun-filled courtyard near the top of Ürgüp's fascinating Cavern Hill. The rooms, furnished with kilims and carpets from Cappadocia, keep many authentic details such as carved ornaments, niches and winepresses, whose origins are lost in remotest antiquity. The lounge/restaurant is a treasure trove of hidden recesses and whimsically fashioned interior spaces. Rented as part of the same establishment is the Mary Hall cave house next door – possibly the cosiest private home we have come across in all Turkey.

rooms	11 + 1: 10 twins/doubles, 1 suite. House for 2-4.
price	140 YTL. Suite 630 YTL. Singles 110 YTL. House 270 YTL.
meals	30-45 YTL, with wine.
closed	Never.
directions	In Ürgüp: Nevşehir exit, right at Club Ürgüp/Turasan Winery.
airport	65km from Kayseri Airport.

	Faruk Maden
tel	+90 (384) 3413173
fax	+90 (384) 3416269
email	faruk@urgupevi.com.tr
web	www.urgupevi.com.tr

Guest house & Self-catering

Map 3 & 6 Entry 162

Photo Nişanyan Gezi Tanitim Ltd, Selçuk, Turkey

north of ankara

north of ankara: historic and remote towns

The region that lies in a broad arch north of Ankara, reaching from Bursa and Kütahya to Tokat, includes some of the finest examples of Turkish vernacular architecture to survive. The old burghers' houses (*konak*) are built of plastered wood and have projecting upper floors, elegantly proportioned windows and red tiled roofs. Most are divided into a public and a private section (*selamlık* and *harem*); many display extravagant carvings.

Safranbolu was the first town in the region to discover the potential of its architectural heritage. Amasya followed suit in the 1990s, and Kastamonu, Beypazarı, Mudurnu and Göynük have joined the bandwagon in the last couple of years.

Old Ankara belongs to this region, too. Behind its oppressively modern façade, the national capital hides a little-known Old Town of considerable charm. Our selection of Ankara hotels includes a delightful *konak*-hotel in the old quarter and a luxurious small hotel in the modern centre.

Angora House

Kalekapısı Sok. 16, 06240 Ankara

As the capital of Turkey flaunts its oppressive modernity, few people realise that there is also an Old Ankara – a hilltop citadel girdled by Byzantine walls and strewn with Roman foundations, next to an old bazaar that rivals the best in the land for local colours and scents. Long a slum, it is now being discovered for what it is, the only part of Ankara that is worth exploring. Several nostalgia-imbued restaurants have led the gentrification and this beautiful period hotel joins them, breathing new life into the old neighbourhood. Muammer and Ahmet are the remarkably gracious hosts whom the diplomatic community of the capital has known for many years as their favourite carpet-dealers. They actually demolished their carpet business to build this dream house – a 19th-century mansion they renovated with love and a precise feeling for detail. The interior is decorated in warm colours and antique furnishings. The atmosphere is friendly and full of flattering touches. And breakfast is nothing short of magnificent.

rooms	6 twins/doubles.
price	100 YTL. Singles 65 YTL.
meals	Restaurants nearby.
closed	November–February.
directions	In Ankara: in the old citadel.
airport	24km from Ankara Airport.

Muammer Uslu & Ahmet Bürtür
tel   +90 (312) 3098380
fax   +90 (312) 3098381

Guest house

Map 2 Entry 163

Gordion Hotel

Tunalı Hilmi Cad. Büklüm Sok. 59, Kavaklıdere, 06660 Ankara

A small luxury hotel conveniently sited in the modern hub of Ankara, within a stone's throw of the capital's principal points of bureaucratic interest, the ministry buildings and the embassies. Unsurprisingly, the fashionable shopping venues and the best restaurants are also within walking distance. Opened a couple of years ago, Gordion Hotel pioneered a trend towards smaller, high-quality accommodations in a city otherwise addicted to the ruthless logic of the barracks. The lobby impresses with its marble-lined opulence and there is a comfortable English-style lobby bar with genuine leather chesterfield armchairs. Bedrooms are richly upholstered in expensive textiles and furnished with brand-new leather-topped desks, gold-plated mirror frames and brass chandeliers – you probably know the kind of atmosphere. In the basement there is a serious indoor pool and a sauna, plus state-of-the-art exercise equipment. The excellent roof restaurant commands a fine bird's-eye view of the city.

rooms	45: 42 twins/doubles, 3 suites.
price	250 YTL. Suites 360–540 YTL. Singles from 195 YTL.
meals	45–60 YTL, with wine.
closed	Never.
directions	In Ankara: near Parliament and US Embassy.
airport	30km from Ankara Airport.

	Savaş Çolakoğlu
tel	+90 (312) 4278080
fax	+90 (312) 4278085
email	efidan@gordionhotel.com
web	www.gordionhotel.com

Hotel

Map 2 Entry 164

Mevalar House
06730 Beypazarı, Ankara

Off any possible itinerary unless you live in Ankara and yearn for a weekend out, Beypazarı comes as a delightful discovery. The outskirts are deceptive. The old centre, huddled in the shadow of a razor-sharp rock, is a lovely collection of cobbled alleys, half-timbered *konaks* and quaint shops untouched by modern gloss. With over 2,500 registered historic houses, the architectural heritage easily surpasses that of the more famous Safranbolu. A mild revival of sorts has been going on here since the beginning of the decade: houses on the main square are given a facelift; a women's market specialising in traditional printed cloths is patched together; some old *konaks* are converted into local-style restaurants. Of the three guest houses opened since 2002, Mevalar Konağı is the best-equipped in terms of comforts and facilities and some of the bedrooms have their own bathrooms. It occupies a wonderful old mansion on the old town square, right at the hub of things – and there's a café downstairs.

rooms	4 twins/doubles, some with own bath or shower.
price	40 YTL.
meals	Restaurants nearby.
closed	Never.
directions	In Beypazarı: town centre.
airport	150km from Ankara Airport.

	Yakup Türkoğlu
tel	+90 (312) 7623698

Hacı Abdullahlar Residence

Seyrancık Mah. Karaarslan Sok. 3, 14800 Mudurnu, Bolu

Mudurnu is a pretty historic town poised on the verge of being 'discovered'. Set in a lushly green valley, the centre is hemmed in by mountains and hardly touched by modern concrete at all. There are some lovely old neighbourhoods by the river; the bazaar is a delight to stroll through. Within an hour's drive lie some of the most idyllic mountain landscapes of western Turkey. Several historic *konaks* have been converted into hotels in the last few years and more are certain to follow. Among the existing ones, the Hacı Abdullahs' House appears to us to be the best prepared to receive guests. It is a stately old house, comfortable but without frills, redolent of a lifestyle now vanished from the deep Turkish province. Mr Uslupat is an engineer and a politician of the old-fashioned Republican stamp; Mrs Uslupat is the local pharmacist. They treat their inn with the excitement of children with of a newfound toy and enjoy sharing a cup of tea with every one of their – not very numerous – guests.

rooms	7 twins/doubles, some with own bath or shower.
price	70 YTL. Singles 50 YTL.
meals	20-30 YTL.
closed	Never.
directions	In Mudurnu: opposite Belediye (Town Hall).

	Osman & Nurcan Uslupat
tel	+90 (374) 4212284
fax	+90 (374) 4212512
email	haciabdullahlar@hotmail.com

Guest house

Map 2 Entry 166

Değirmenyeri Mountain Houses
Dağ Mvk. (PK 1), Kilözü, 14800 Mudurnu, Bolu

The hill country south of Bolu is an area of flawless rural beauty. Bright green meadows spread around the fenced cattle farms; dark firs alternate with leafy woods that turn a dazzling red in October. A pretty mountain road, more like Vermont than Turkey, branches off from the halfway point of the Ankara-Istanbul motorway to Lake Abant; it continues to Mudurnu on the softer, and less travelled, south side of the mountain. Değirmenyeri ('Millplace') Houses fit the landscape well. They hide in a fold of the hills near a village smelling of cow dung and fresh grass. It is not a hotel in the professional sense but rather a cluster of comfortable cottages set in a farm garden inhabited by chickens, ducks, goats, cats and a friendly St Bernard. The buildings are of wood and stone; the furnishings, a mix of Turkish old and new, vary. Your hosts are an urban couple who knew city life was over for them the day they stumbled upon this faraway valley. They listen to jazz and classical music, cook superbly, serve it well, and enjoy chatting around the fireplace in the evening.

rooms	5 cottages for 5.
price	Half board 110 YTL. Singles from 55 YTL.
meals	Half board only.
closed	Never.
directions	8km from Mudurnu: Abant/Bolu road for 2km; left towards Kilözü; past forestry depot.

	Ulvi & Tülay Ilgaz
tel	+90 (374) 4212677
fax	+90 (374) 4212688
web	www.degirmenyeri.com

Guest house

Map 2 Entry 167

Selvili Köşk

Çeşme Mah. Mescid Sok. 23, 67700 Safranbolu, Karabük

Safranbolu is a museum-town that preserves some of the most beautiful surviving examples of traditional Turkish civil architecture. Clinging to the slopes of a ravine, the old town is full of stately half-timbered mansions (*konaks*) seemingly bypassed by the 20th century. Half of them moulder gently, owned by the impoverished descendants of original owners, or more often by their servants and doorkeepers. More than 40 have been revived within the last decade and turned into small hotels of remarkable charm and character. One of the prettiest of Safranbolu's *konak*-hotels carries the name of the century-old cypress (*selvi*) gracing its front yard. Renovated thoroughly in the 1990s, the house retains many details and much of the spirit of the original, built in 1883. The reception hall has a five-metre high ceiling of spectacularly fine detail. Most of the bedrooms are a good size and rejoice in elaborate dark-wood wall-to-wall cabinetry and wraparound divans on which you may recline and gaze out of large old-style windows.

rooms	7 twins/doubles.
price	70 YTL. Singles 50 YTL.
meals	Restaurants nearby.
closed	Never.
directions	In Safranbolu: near the main square.
airport	230km from Ankara Airport.

İsmail Karabudak

tel	+90 (370) 7128646
fax	+90 (370) 7252294

Guest house

Map 2 Entry 168

Paşa & Gökçüoğlu Residences

Çarşı Mah. Kalealtı Sok. 1-17, 67700 Safranbolu, Karabük

The original owner of this sober and beautifully proportioned 18th-century home was Izzet Mehmed Pasha, prime minister to Selim III who retired to Safranbolu after failing to stop Bonaparte in Egypt. Two halves of his former house belong to two rival owners who, thankfully for us, have at last agreed on a single management to run it as a hotel. The rooms are wonderful and the large garden is an absolute boon in Safranbolu; make the most of its cherries, figs and plums at breakfast. And bring slippers for indoors – the carpets are antique and are cleaned every day! Another part of the same establishment is a beautiful summer *konak* in the garden suburb of Bağlar. This is a magnificent house full of the poignant details of a vanished way of life. (Note the cat corridor in the granary, built to deter mice, and the intricate patterns of the bedroom ceilings that were apparently designed to ward off insomnia.) It's usually reserved for organised groups that need no chaperoning but see if you can talk your way into having it all to yourself: fun to be grand vizier for a day.

rooms	18 twins/doubles.
price	101 YTL. Singles 85 YTL.
meals	30-45 YTL, with wine.
closed	Never.
directions	In Safranbolu: near the main square.
airport	230km from Ankara Airport.

	Özlem Urgancıoğlu
tel	+90 (370) 7128153
fax	+90 (370) 7121073
email	info@safranboluturizm.com.tr
web	www.safranboluturizm.com.tr

Guest house

Map 2 Entry 169

Touring Club Hotel

Hacı Halil Mah. Çelik Gülersoy Cad. 18, 67700 Safranbolu, Karabük

One of the finest old *konaks* of Safranbolu, the Asmazlar House, features a basin of cut stone in the middle of its upper-floor reception room. It is the epitome of the traditional Ottoman art of fine living: one can imagine turbanned gentlemen reclining on the divans that run round the pool, picking cooled grapes from the water. The Touring Club's Havuzlu Konak (Pool Mansion) is a replica of that marvel of 18th-century technology. It is an impressive old house decorated in a compromise between the traditionally sober Turkish manner and the more ornate quasi-Victorian style favoured by Mr Gülersoy, the late aristocratic director of the Club. The pool is the centrepiece of a café where old Turkish music is performed live on most evenings. A second historic house, the Walnut Tree Mansion, shares the same garden; together thay make up the hotel. The renovating sweep, which has worked such wonders with Touring's better-known Istanbul properties, was expected to reach this provincial gem at the time of writing.

rooms	23: 18 twins/doubles, 5 suites for 5.
price	100 YTL. Suites 120 YTL. Singles 75 YTL.
meals	30-45 YTL, with wine.
closed	November-March.
directions	In Safranbolu: near the main square.
airport	230km from Ankara Airport.

Enver Temel

tel	+90 (370) 7252883
fax	+90 (370) 7123824
email	safranbolu@turing.org.tr

Hotel

Map 2 Entry 170

Raşitler Garden House

Bağlar Mah. Değirmenbaşı 65 , 78600 Safranbolu, Karabük

In the good old days the well-to-do of Safranbolu used to keep a winter home in town and a summer home in the suburbs. Some of the finest old *konaks* of Safranbolu are actually to be found in the garden suburb of Bağlar (Orchards), about three kilometres up the hill from the centre, though most modern-day visitors miss this bit completely. The Raşitler House stands in a particularly green corner of Bağlar, next to the old public watermill. It is a stately and sober old house, renovated in good conservative taste by the current owner, a retired air force officer with a friendly glint in his eye. The interior features all the heart-warming details of a 1900s' house – overstuffed sofas with hand-embroidered arm-sleeves, walnut tables from before the Great War and faded sepia family photos. Rooms are smallish and the bathrooms have been ingeniously squeezed into cupboards. A big plus is the large and peaceful garden shaded by an old walnut tree.

rooms	5 twins/doubles.
price	90-100 YTL. Singles from 50 YTL.
meals	Meals by arrangement.
closed	Never.
directions	2km from Safranbolu: up to the Bağlar district, left at main junction.
airport	230km from Ankara Airport.

	Erhan Hangün
tel	+90 (370) 7251345
fax	+90 (370) 7251345

Guest house

Map 2 Entry 171

Yörük Pansiyon
Yörük, Safranbolu, Karabük

If touristified authenticism leaves you cold, here is authenticity of the purest sort. Yörük is the secret twin of Safranbolu, offering some 140 beautiful Ottoman houses in their crumbling and unrestored splendour without one nasty new building in sight. It used to be a substantial town; now it is reduced to a quasi-derelict village in a beautiful setting of unkempt gardens and overgrown mulberry orchards. There is a grocery, which is sometimes open, and a couple of ad hoc eateries catering to a meagre weekend traffic in summer. The only accommodation in town is this magnificent old house which offers utterly basic hospitality in its four rooms. The rooms are not entirely free of peeling plaster, though they have wonderful 60cm-wide floorboards, intricate built-in cabinetry and many spirits lurking in the cupboards. There is one Turkish-style squat loo. But the family in charge conveys the feeling that they genuinely enjoy sharing their food and their home with a visitor.

rooms	4 twins/doubles, sharing shower and one wc.
price	60 YTL. Singles 30 YTL.
meals	Meals by arrangement.
closed	Occasionally in winter.
directions	11km from Safranbolu: toward Kastamonu 11km; left to Yörük centre, 1km.

	Necati Erdem
tel	+90 (370) 7372153

Guest house

Map 2 Entry 172

Toprakçılar Konakları

İsmailbey Mah. Alemdar Sok. 2, 37100 Kastamonu

Kastamonu is the epitome of a conservative Anatolian city: its bazaar district, laced and woven with scores of minor medieval monuments, oozes the look and feel of olden times. The historic neighbourhoods below the castle are full of stately old homes in various stages of decay, while the Mosque of Mahmut Bey, a 14th-century jewel, stands a few miles outside the town. This pair of pretty houses, revived in 2003, represent the first – and so far only – serious attempt to bring tourism to Kastamonu. Mrs Kırbaş is an art historian and travel agency director from Istanbul who fell in love with the city and proceeded to invest in it as an act of the heart. From the outside, the houses are a delight to look at; the interiors, too, offer a comfortable and cosy atmosphere. A team of local ladies works wonders in the kitchen and the restaurant is one of the very few places in deeply conservative Kastamonu where you can have a sinful glass of *rakı* with your dinner.

rooms	10: 3 twins/doubles, 6 triples, 1 suite for 4.
price	100-180 YTL. Singles from 60 YTL.
meals	20-30 YTL.
closed	Never.
directions	In Kastamonu: near İsmailbey Mosque in city centre.

	Gülsen Kırbaş
tel	+90 (366) 2121812
fax	+90 (366) 2128312
email	info@toprakcilar.com
web	www.toprakcilar.com

Guest house

Map 2 Entry 173

Photo Nişanyan Gezi Tanitim Ltd, Selçuk, Turkey

black sea

...but green mountains

In landscape and history the Black Sea coast differs from the rest of Turkey. A high range of mountains blocks access to the interior, while high rainfall throughout the year supports jungle-like vegetation.

Two points are worth bearing in mind when planning a trip. First, the east is a better bet than the west; all of the memorable destinations, in fact, lie east of Trabzon and Rize. Second, the mountains are more interesting than the coast, each upper valley being a secret world unto itself.

Only two small towns in this region have anything to offer the tourist: Uzungöl, which wraps itself around a beautiful lake, and Ayder, a launch pad for the fascinating region of the Hemşin and the Kaçkar Mountains. There are some interesting small places to stay near the clifftop monastery of Sumela, though we have yet to find one suitable for this guide.

The fascinating province of Artvin — worth at least a week's exploration — offers three basic guest houses in remote spots that will linger in your memory a long, long time.

İlk Pansiyon

Gümüşlü Mah. Hitit Sok. 1, 05100 Amasya

This old Armenian mansion in the centre of Amasya has been lovingly renovated by your host, an architect who has dedicated himself to saving the historic heritage of this beautiful city. His ground-floor office doubles as the headquarters of an international programme of urban renewal sponsored by a Japanese university and supported by European funds. Loyal guests at the *pansiyon* include academics, explorers and journalists from far-flung corners of the globe who return, often, to enjoy this unlikely Noah's ark in the middle of remote Anatolia. The house is set in a flagstone-paved courtyard protected by high garden walls and what it lacks in comfort it makes up for in charm and atmosphere. Each room is priced differently, each is understatedly appealing. Best of all are numbers 3 and 5 – large, many-windowed halls with creaky floors and indoor baths that hide, in old Turkish fashion, behind built-in cabinetry. Equally delightful is the garden room with its own little trellised courtyard.

rooms	6: 2 twins/doubles, 2 family rooms for 2-4, 2 family rooms for 3-5.
price	50-85 YTL. Singles from 32 YTL.
meals	20-30 YTL.
closed	Never.
directions	In Amasya: on left bank, opposite Tourist Information Bureau.

	Ali Kamil Yalçın
tel	+90 (358) 2181689
fax	+90 (358) 2186277

Guest house

Map 3 Entry 174

Emin Efendi Pansiyon

Hatuniye Mah. Hazeranlar Sok. 73, 05100 Amasya

A 200 year-old Ottoman house in the historic part of Amasya, set on the bank of the river Yeşilırmak — almost like a Bosphorus *yalı* or a palazzo by the Grand Canal — below the rock tombs of the ancient Pontic kings. The view across the river takes in the classic silhouette of the 15th-century mosque of Sultan Bayezid. It is a friendly, unpretentious house that has more the character of an old-fashioned Anatolian home than a normal hotel. The flagstone-paved courtyard has a pergola of grapevine where neighbourhood ladies often sit and gossip. In the main house you get two rooms per floor with a shared bathroom, high painted ceilings, Turkish-style divans all around and huge wall-to-wall windows that open directly onto the river. The cellar has been converted into a living room with a fireplace and a piano. The former gatekeeper's room, perched quaintly over the garden gate, is a separate guestroom with its own en suite facilities.

rooms	5 triples, one with own bathroom.
price	80 YTL. Singles 50 YTL.
meals	20-30 YTL.
closed	Never.
directions	In Amasya: on the right bank below the royal tombs.

	Gülseval Özkök Yücer
tel	+90 (358) 2120852
fax	+90 (358) 2122552

Guest house

Map 3 Entry 175

Grand Pasha Hotel

Hatuniye Mah. Tevfik Hafız çıkmazı 5, 05100 Amasya

Another wonderful old house set directly on the riverbank in the heart of historic Amasya — easily the most attractive of all Anatolian cities. It lies in a gorge of the Yeşilırmak ('Green River'), hemmed in by great limestone cliffs that have constricted urban growth and pushed new development to the outskirts of the city. The left bank of the river forms a narrow ledge on which a row of pretty Ottoman houses stand with their upper storeys jutting out over the river. Over them hang the massive rock tombs of the kings of ancient Pontus. Scores of attractive Turkish monuments date from the age when the town was the capital of a succession of medieval Turkish emirates. Intricately detailed and painted, the two upper-floor bedrooms of the Grand Pasha Hotel are hard to beat; the ground-floor rooms are more modest. The fact that each room has its own en suite bathroom is also a plus. Our only gripe is the nightly entertainment noise from neighbouring establishments.

rooms	9: 8 twins/doubles, 1 suite.
price	60 YTL. Suite 90 YTL. Singles 35 YTL.
meals	20-30 YTL.
closed	Never.
directions	In Amasya: on the right bank below the royal tombs.

	Eray Soyalp, Burhan Bayrak
tel	+90 (358) 2124158
fax	+90 (358) 2186269
email	grandpashaotel@kolayweb.com

Guest house

Map 3 Entry 176

Ardıçlı Dağ Evi
Ardıçlı, Niksar, Tokat

A charming mountain lodge in a faraway place where you least expect it to find such things. Niksar – and the valley of the Kelkit generally – is probably the last undiscovered touring frontier in the country. Ardıçlı is a hill village set high above Niksar, all green and cool and with a splendid view of the valley below. If you happen to be passing by, it is well worth driving the extra 13km into this bit of deepest Turkey. The hosts are an elderly, engaging country doctor and his wife, who does wonders in the kitchen. They have two houses next to each other, built in modern chalet style with a lot of sturdy sense but few traditional touches. Each has four guest rooms sharing one bathroom and a comfortable lounge. A guest is normally given a whole house, so he won't share with strangers. Niksar's name echoes the Roman Neocaesaria, where St Gregory the Thaumaturge once performed his many miracles. Monuments of a Turkish dynasty that flourished here in the 12th century fill the town.

rooms	2 houses for 8, each house with one bathroom.
price	40 YTL per person.
meals	Meals by arrangement.
closed	Never.
directions	13km from Niksar: on the road up towards Ünye.

Şehsuvar & Nevber Savuran
tel   +90 (356) 5421242

Guest house

Map 3 Entry 177

İnan Hotel

Uzungöl, 61960 Çaykara, Trabzon

Uzungöl, meaning long lake, is the ultimate beauty spot of the Black Sea
mountains. It has meadows and forest and a smiling all-timber village.
Spectacularly untamed highlands lie within driving distance. Thirty years ago, no
outsider ever came here. Now a small resort of some two dozen chalet-style
hotels has grown around the lake, retailing the joys of fresh air, fresh trout and
some typically eccentric regional flair. The villagers, devout Muslims to a man,
speak the Pontic dialect of Greek. İnan Hotel is the oldest and most comfortable
of the lot. Mr İnan is a philosopher of regional fame and his apophthegms, full of
startling insights into the human condition and a deep religious respect for nature,
cover the walls of his establishment. Despite commercial success, the hotel keeps
a genuine feel, and the daughters, who run the place, are delightful. No plastic,
and few traces of cement, mar the family-style wooden chalets or the newer,
comfortably fitted hotel wing. The food is famously good, though Mr İnan does
not believe in serving alcohol.

rooms	43: 18 twins/doubles, 25 cabins.
price	90 YTL. Cabins 70 YTL for 2. Singles from 65 YTL.
meals	20-30 YTL.
closed	Never.
directions	45km from Of; turn inland at Of; to Uzungöl via Çaykara.
airport	95km from Trabzon Airport.

	Dursun Ali İnan
tel	+90 (462) 6566021
fax	+90 (462) 6566066

Hotel

Map 7 Entry 178

Fırtına Pansiyon

Şenyuva (Şinçiva), 53750 Çamlıhemşin, Rize

The western branch of the Fırtına River flows through an enchanted valley — a wild and mysterious land that seems to belong to some mythical northern clime. It is possible to walk seven kilometres from Şenyuva to the Zil Fortress without meeting another living soul. Waterfalls come tumbling out of every clearing in the forest; ancient mansions built of solid chestnut lie hidden in the fog higher up the cliffs. They are mostly abandoned and covered in moss. Fırtına Pension, converted from the old schoolhouse of Şenyuva village, lies by the thundering river at the end of the paved road. The old classroom serves as a sitting and dining hall while the teachers' quarters have become five pleasantly furnished and cosy rooms, with a kitchen open to all. In addition, there are two timber cabins used mostly by mountain climbers, and a lovely new house. Selçuk and his sister have come back to the land of their birth after city careers in teaching. They offer good conversation, good food and good rakı to a fairly literate circle of guests.

rooms	7 + 1: 5 twins/doubles, 2 cabins for 4, some with own bath or shower. 1 house for 4.
price	Half board 35 YTL per person.
meals	Half board only.
closed	November-February.
directions	6km from Çamlıhemşin: upriver and right (poor road).
airport	150km from Trabzon Airport.

	Selçuk & Rukiye Güney
tel	+90 (464) 6533111
email	firtinavadisi@hotmail.com
web	www.firtinavadisi.com

Guest house & Self-catering

Map 7 Entry 179

Cancik Hotel

Çat, 53750 Çamlıhemşin, Rize

A very basic and utterly charming inn at the far end of Turkey's most spectacular mountain valley. The lobby acts as road stop, general store and gossip parlour all at once. It is decorated with antediluvian liquor bottles, is filled with the sweet smell of sooty pinewood and hosts a remarkable cast of eccentric and loquacious mountain men at all hours of the day. The usual fare is a superb *muhlama*, a cheese and cornmeal fondue that is the highland speciality. A wonderful little terrace hangs out over the mountain brook that roars past with a deafening boom. The wood-panelled bedrooms upstairs have absolutely no frills; somewhat better are the newer bungalow-style accommodations built on the pasture behind. The air is shrouded in mist for most of the time; when it parts, it reveals the snow-capped peaks of Tatos (3,560m) to the east and Verçenik (3,711m) to the west. The village (20 dwellings, one mosque) is at the parting of the roads for the two mountains, and a popular stop on the trek up to the summer pastures.

rooms	9: 7 twins/doubles, 2 cabins for 4, some with own bath or shower.
price	Half board 80 YTL. Singles from 40 YTL.
meals	Half board only.
closed	November–March.
directions	28km from Çamlıhemşin: 16km past Zilkale (poor road).
airport	170km from Trabzon Airport.

	Rasim, Zeki, Tahsin Mafratoğlu
tel	+90 (464) 6544120

Guest house

Map 7 Entry 180

Kuşpuni
Ayder, 53760 Çamlıhemşin, Rize

After a lifetime spent as a surgeon in the big city, Dr Veziroğlu came back to his native mountains with his wife and grown children to build this comfortable little hotel near the hot springs of Ayder. Kuşpuni means a bird's nest in the local dialect. In due course, as mayor of Çamlıhemşin, he helped steer the village away from the chaotic rush of the early 1990s towards the more nature-friendly, soft-toned resort that it is today. All power to his arm. Dinner is rich in local specialities such as *muhlama* (a fondue of cheese, butter and cornmeal), cornbread and a variety of unusual vegetables. Rooms in the main building are decked out in frilly bedspreads and centrally heated – a boon during the cold highland nights. There is also a nice old *serender* – a timber storehouse built on stilts in the regional style – with two unheated, very basic rooms of greater character. Mrs Veziroğlu presides over the house with motherly instinct and charm.

rooms	18: 16 twins/doubles, 2 suites for 5.
price	100 YTL. Suites 120 YTL. Singles 60 YTL.
meals	20-30 YTL.
closed	Occasionally in winter.
directions	17km from Çamlıhemşin: in Ayder village.
airport	160km from Trabzon Airport.

	Refah & Manolya Veziroğlu
tel	+90 (464) 6572052
fax	+90 (464) 6572205

Guest house

Map 7 Entry 181

Serender Pansiyon

Ayder, 53760 Çamlıhemşin, Rize

Hemşin is a land of perpetual mist and snow-capped mountains, and Ayder is its tourist hub. It already had some local fame as a thermal spa before it started attracting the climbers and the trekkers from the big city, and it rivals the best of Swiss villages for the beauty of its setting. It lies 1,300m high in a steep valley where a dozen waterfalls tumble down from the cliffs on all sides and evergreens grow to unusual heights. About 20 all-timber chalets (and a few unsightly *beton*-palaces from the 1980s) provide the accommodation. Serender Pension is the homeliest and in some ways the most comfortable of the lot. It has wood-panelled rooms in sauna style, some of which are quite big and some of which interconnect to make family suites. There is a nice terrace looking onto a perfectly idyllic landscape of wild waterfalls, emerald pastures, happy cows and Hemşinese women in resplendent local costume. Above all there is Mrs Mamus herself, a magnificently talkative woman with sparkling eyes who serves a breakfast feast.

rooms	14 twins/doubles/triples.
price	50 YTL. Singles 25 YTL.
meals	Meals by arrangement.
closed	December–April.
directions	17km from Çamlıhemşin: in Ayder village.
airport	160km from Trabzon Airport.

	Tenzile Mamus
tel	+90 (464) 6572201

Guest house

Map 7 Entry 182

Karahan Pansiyon

Altıparmak (Barhal), 08820 Yusufeli, Artvin

Barhal is a remote and beautiful village built in a forest valley of fabulous exuberance at the southern foot of Mount Kaçkar. Along with Hevek, further up, it is one of two bases for climbing Turkey's finest peak and the starting point for the two-day trek across the mountain to Çamlıhemşin. You reach there by a difficult road that follows a wild brook – beware, it gets wilder as you climb. A medieval cathedral, a massive 10th-century edifice with a strangely 'modern' angular look, stands unreally in the village clearing. Karahan Pension consists of two wooden chalets in Artvin's traditional rambling style. The ground-floor rooms are poor; the surprise is the half-covered roof terrace, huge and invitingly decked out with kilims and cushions. Fifteen or 20 can easily sleep there on floor bedding of heavy natural wool and impeccably white linen. The hospitality of Mehmet Karahan and his sons is of the sort that brings tears to the eyes on departure, and solemn vows of speedy return.

rooms	6 twins/doubles + roof terrace for 15.
price	Half board 38 YTL. Singles 19 YTL.
meals	Half board only.
closed	November–April.
directions	26km from Yusufeli: via Sarıgöl to Altıparmak/Barhal (poor road).
airport	230km from Erzurum Airport.

	Mehmet Karahan
tel	+90 (466) 8262071
fax	+90 (466) 8262014

Guest house

Map 7 Entry 183

Laşet Restaurant & Motel

Ardahan Yolu, 08700 Şavşat , Artvin

The pastures are so green, one feels envy for the cows. An amazing variety of wildflowers invades them in summer, covering the hills in fantastic blankets of pink, purple and azure. Villages are full of wooden chalets with elaborate balconies; forests of tall dark fir frame the hills. The Yalnızçam Pass, at 2,200m, is the last of the mountain passes to join the lush valleys of the Black Sea to the desolate highlands of the interior; it is also, arguably, the most spectacular. Standing 14km before the pass on the Artvin side, Laşet is the perfect place to stop for a final farewell as you come to the end of your Black Sea grand tour. Their grill-and-*rakı* restaurant is reputed to be the best in the area. Their wood-panelled rooms, added in 2004, offer a clean and comfortable bed but nothing fancier. The name refers to a mineral water spring nearby; it apparently means 'bitter water' in the local Georgian dialect – but the hospitality is as sweet as you might wish.

rooms	6 twins/doubles.
price	50 YTL. Singles from 25 YTL.
meals	20-30 YTL.
closed	Never.
directions	8km from Şavşat: on Ardahan road.
airport	120km from Kars Airport.

	Metecem Çelik
tel	+90 (466) 5712136
fax	+90 (466) 5171226

Guest house

Map 8 Entry 184

Karagöl Pansiyon
Karagöl Mvk., Meşeli, 08700 Şavşat, Artvin

We were amazed to find this very basic but reasonably comfortable *pansiyon* in what is probably the remotest piece of wilderness in all Turkey. The setting is mind-blowingly beautiful. Originally a lodging for the Forest Administration, it was privatised and taken up by a latter-day hermit with a political past. Babo does not necessarily like all guests, nor does he believe in excessive service, though when the mood is right he is the most fascinating of hosts in the old school of chivalry. He has had a surprising turnover of travellers attracted by the spectacular beauty of the place and the endless possibilities of exploration. In summer the forest is full of brown bear, wild boar, fox and deer. In autumn swarms of wild geese cover the surface of Karagöl Lake. The upper valleys of Şavşat look more like the Swiss Alps than any other place in Turkey and villages consist purely of timber chalets with finely ornamented balconies in the local style. The ruins of a monumental Georgian cathedral of the 10th century can be seen in a neighbouring village.

rooms	6 twins/doubles, two with own bath or shower.
price	Low/negociable.
meals	Meals by arrangement.
closed	Never.
directions	27km from Şavşat: Artvin road 2km, then right to Veliköy (poor road).
airport	155km from Kars Airport.

	Atanur Şahin (Babo)
tel	+90 (466) 5372137
fax	+90 (466) 5171260

Photo Turkish Culture & Tourism Office

east & southeast

the fascinating east

A region of vast and lonely volcanic highlands whose exotic medieval cities have a 'Middle Eastern' feel. Spectacular monuments of ancient and forgotten cultures stand in remote places, seldom disturbed by the tourist coach.

The region's tourism, never more than a trickle, was brought to a complete standstill by the Kurdish troubles of the 1990s and, again, by the Iraqi disaster of the 2000s. Consider this a good thing! There is no security risk to speak of — as far as petty crime goes, the east is safer than the west, the roads aren't bad and there are plenty of decent if unexciting hotels in the major towns.

Our favourite places are Mardin and Midyat and the fascinating heartlands of old Syriac culture that lie around them. Urfa stands out for its amazing bazaar, while the mountain country around Lake Van abounds in seldom-visited medieval monasteries and castles. The great mountain top sanctuary of Nemrut Dağı is awesome in itself, though saddled with visitors in summer.

Anatolia Houses

Köroğlu Sok. 6, Şahinbey, 27400 Gaziantep

Your host Timur is part Turkish, part American and altogether outside the common mould. Tired of being an executive in the music industry, he went on a motorcycle tour of the world, decided Gaziantep was the greatest place under the sun, bought some lovely old mansions gone to seed, and turned them into this wonderfully stylish period hotel which is now one of the chief reasons why anyone should want to travel this far. His enthusiasm is infectious. Symphony orchestras have gone to perform in Anatolia Houses at Timur's invitation, and European Union bigshots have come to check reports of a strange cultural vitality gripping this remote Turkish corner. The hotel consists of three houses in the austere black-and-white architecture of Old Antep. The bedrooms are cool and airy, furnished sparsely with the restrained elegance of a man of good taste; the smaller house serves as a luxury suite. Ceilings are lofty, floors carry the original tiles. The location is the heart of what remains of the old town of Gaziantep, and the bazaar starts around the corner.

rooms	13: 10 twins/doubles, 3 suites.
price	135 YTL. Suites 170 YTL. Singles from 100 YTL.
meals	Meals by arrangement.
closed	Never.
directions	In Gaziantep: near the fortress, opposite İmam Çağdaş restaurant.
airport	20km from Gaziantep Airport.

	Timur Schindel
tel	+90 (342) 2209525
fax	+90 (342) 2209528
email	info@anadoluevleri.com
web	www.anadoluevleri.com

Hotel

Map 6 Entry 186

Antik Belkıs Han

Kayacık Ara Sok. 16, Şahinbey, 27400 Gaziantep

A charming, quirky and very personal house hidden in an unexpected corner of central Antep's urban clutter. The building is a splendid old stone house of the type that has almost disappeared from this once-beautiful city. It was saved from the wrecking squad and refurbished in loving detail by Ms Karabiber, a painter, activist and businesswoman of infectious vivacity. Her house combines the charm of a European country inn with a personal warmth that is perhaps more typical of this part of the world. Her breakfasts are a feast to the eye and the palate and there's a room lined with books on the top floor. Gaziantep takes pride in being the 'Paris of the East': a modern, wealthy, businesslike city without the medieval flair of other south-eastern towns. It is not strong on atmosphere, which may be exactly what one needs for a while when too much atmosphere threatens to overwhelm. Regional food and Turkish wines are served in the cellar restaurant/bar – and beyond; Gaziantep food is famously good. More memorably, the city is the acknowledged baklava capital of the world.

rooms	5 twins/doubles, some with own bath or shower.
price	95 YTL. Singles 70 YTL.
meals	25 YTL.
closed	15 November–15 March.
directions	In Gaziantep: behind main Post Office.
airport	20km from Gaziantep Airport.

	Mizyal Karabiber Nacaroglu
tel	+90 (342) 2311084
fax	+90 (342) 3600880
email	mizyal@hotmail.com
web	www.belkishan.com

Guest house

Map 6 Entry 187

Gülizar Guesthouse

İrfaniye Sok. 22, 63200 Urfa

This is not a hotel in the usual sense at all but a banqueting house in deep south-eastern style where you can choose to sleep after a particularly exhausting dinner, should you wish. The setting is a beautiful old stone mansion arranged Syrian-style around a courtyard and decorated gorgeously in the traditional manner. Dinner is served in private rooms where you eat reclining on cushions like the ancient Greeks and Arabs. The service is old-fashioned and courteous, in a manner that is no longer familiar to the less feudal parts of the country. Then you snap your fingers, the table is transported away and the floor beds come rolling out of the cupboard. These are wonderfully comfortable floor beds of genuine wool and generous size, and the sleeping rooms give a very real sense of what daily life in the ancient East must have been like. One drawback is that they serve no alcohol here; another is that there is only one bathroom, and that is downstairs.

rooms	8 twins/doubles sharing one bathroom.
price	70 YTL.
meals	20-30 YTL.
closed	Never.
directions	In Urfa: between Water Square and Earth Square.
airport	10km from Urfa Airport.

	Ali Beyazkuş
tel	+90 (414) 2150505
fax	+90 (414) 2163839
web	www.gulizarkonukevi.com

Guest house

Map 7 Entry 188

The Governor's Guesthouse

Vali Fuat Cad., 63200 Urfa

The deeply Middle Eastern city of Urfa hides many such mansions in its chaotic labyrinth, sober and grey on the outside and giving no hint of the lovely courtyards within. The Governor's Guesthouse occupies the finest of the lot, the former home – although the official story remains mute on this delicate point – of the Armenian bishop. It was renovated a few years back, went through many ups and downs, and ended up opening to the public as a state guest house. This means you pay a pittance and expect few services in return, though the innate hospitality of the east will often shine through the dusty bureaucratic mask. The interior mixes Governor's Guest style, pompous but cheap, with some impressive antiques. There is a good restaurant downstairs with lots of carpets and floor tables in traditional style. For the treat, however, you have to go up to the flat roof. Here you face the Citadel of Urfa and the Sacred Pool of Abraham, and the bottomless antiquity of the city becomes almost palpable.

rooms	6 twins/doubles.
price	75-90 YTL. Singles from 40 YTL.
meals	10-20 YTL.
closed	Never.
directions	In Urfa centre: near Selahaddin Eyyubi Mosque.
airport	10km from Urfa Airport.

	TC
tel	+90 (414) 2159377
fax	+90 (414) 2149377

Guest house

Map 7 Entry 189

Erdoba Hotel
Birinci Cad. 135, 47100 Mardin

Mardin is an enchanted town – an old Middle Eastern labyrinth full of secrets and surprises. The houses, built in tiers on the side of a steep mountain, look more like castles than homes and are usually large enough for a family of several dozen. The Erdoba Hotel is the first serious attempt to convert the old houses of Mardin to tourist use. It consists of two dwellings. The main one has some impressive public rooms but its bedrooms are rather routine; the second, located a few steep alleys down, is the jewel. It has nine almost palatial rooms preserved exactly as they should be, full of intricately carved stonework and splendid altar-niches in the local fashion. It lies in a secluded courtyard cut off by high walls and a gate that could withstand a minor siege. At night, the Plain of Mesopotamia stretches like a vast illuminated sea as far as Syria. There is no desk and no office at the second house so that it can become a wholly private place if you are there with family and friends.

rooms	29: 26 twins/doubles, 3 suites.
price	120 YTL. Singles from 75 YTL.
meals	10-20 YTL.
closed	Never.
directions	In Mardin centre: on upper main street.
airport	10km from Mardin Airport.

	Müfit Gözü
tel	+90 (482) 2137787
fax	+90 (482) 2128821
email	erdoba@erdoba.com.tr
web	www.erdoba.com.tr

Hotel

Map 7 Entry 190

Midyat Guesthouse
47500 Midyat, Mardin

Architecturally the purest town in all Turkey, Midyat retains a medieval air with its narrow lanes and fortified stone mansions. The old town was peopled until recently by Syriac Christians, who still keep eight active churches. Many of their exquisitely filigreed ancestral houses have been taken over by Kurdish refugees from the ravaged countryside. The only reasonable accommodation in town is the Government (or, properly, the District Prefecture's) guest house which occupies the magnificently showy residence of a former head of the local Protestant community. (Yes, they existed!). No reservations are taken ahead of time but you can usually find room at a moment's notice unless some official bigshot is in town with a large retinue. There is no breakfast, although poor old Nuri, the keeper, will insist on sharing his bread and tea with you and will be on the edge of tears if he fails to please you. The grand room on the top level, with all Midyat under its windows, is possibly the most gorgeous guest room in the country.

rooms	7 twins/doubles.
price	50 YTL.
meals	Restaurants nearby.
closed	Never.
directions	In Midyat Old Town (Midyat proper).
airport	75km from Mardin Airport.

	TC
tel	+90 (482) 4621354
fax	+90 (482) 4622061

Guest house

Map 7 Entry 191

Club Natura Van
Çolpan, 65500 Muradiye, Van

Not having seen a tourist in a decade, Turkey's most beautiful highland lake is now making a – slow – return to the travellers' mainstream. Club Natura's bungalow compound is a mark of things to come: a pioneer camp set up in the middle of nowhere. The position is enchanting: a lonely headland opposite the over-4000-metre volcanic cone of Mount Süpan. The lake is a striking blue and perfectly swimmable if you don't mind the soapy consistency. A vast fruit orchard lies next to the grounds. The silence is overwhelming. The nine rooms are simple and clean, if without many comforts; note that there are further rooms that are not ensuite. Within walking distance is a sub-medieval Kurdish village where the children (hundreds of them!) will treat you as the most exciting thing that ever happened. A short distance further south you find the isle of Adır with its 13th-century church of St George, utterly unknown and unvisited.

rooms	9 twins/doubles.
price	80 YTL. Singles 40 YTL.
meals	Meals by arrangement.
closed	October-June.
directions	60km from Van: off Muradiye road near the north-eastern tip of the lake.
airport	65km from Van Airport.

	Aysel Koch
tel	+90 (432) 2672108
fax	+90 (432) 2672108
email	info@clubnatura.com
web	www.clubnatura.com

Camp

Map 8 Entry 192

History and culture

Three millennia in 3.5 paragraphs...
The difficult thing about Turkey's history is that it has not one but several. Long before it became the home of Muslim Turks, Asia Minor was one of the principal theatres of ancient Greek and Roman civilisation. The earliest Greek philosophers were born in Ionia, on the western coast of present Turkey. Two of the Seven Wonders of the ancient world (the Artemision of Ephesus and the Mausoleion of Halicarnassus) and two of the four most populous cities of the Roman Empire (Antioch and Constantinople) were located in this country. No fewer than 300 ancient Greek and Roman cities in ruins, some explored and packaged for tourism, others lying barely known in faraway locations, remain as testimonies of that era.

Christianity was here, too. Apostles Peter and Paul met in Antioch, modern Antakya, to take the momentous decision to call it a new religion. John proclaimed the pending Apocalypse to the Seven Churches of Asia, which were seven communities of the Roman province of Asia, centred on Ephesus. The Hagia Sophia of Constantinople was the world's largest church until surpassed by St Peter's of Rome 1,000 years later. Greek and Armenian Christians formed nearly a quarter of Turkey's population until the 1910s. Their subsequent disappearance is an event that retains its mystery for the average Turk, who does not generally learn about such matters from his school curriculum.

The Turks first emerged as a nation on the northern frontiers of China. They converted to Islam in the 11th century, and started their great westward push immediately afterward. The first Turkish states were formed in eastern and central Anatolia after 1071. The capture of Constantinople in 1453 completed the Turkish conquest of the country. The Ottoman Empire grew rapidly from a minor Anatolian emirate into the world's largest superpower: at its peak, its frontiers extended from Vienna and Budapest to Algiers, Yemen and the Basra. It went down just as spectacularly, and collapsed at the end of World War I. Twenty independent countries were carved out of its carcass. The Turkish

Photo Turkish Culture and Tourism Office

History and culture

The economy, long a spectacularly unruly affair with inflation averaging 72% a year during the 90s, has taken off brilliantly since 2001. The new lira, introduced in 2005, fuels optimism. On a more mundane level, EU citizens are now entitled to own land freely in every part of the country.

Few seem totally convinced that Turkey will join the EU any time soon, though there is agreement that the effort itself is doing the country a lot of good. Paradoxically, it is the first politically Muslim party to govern Turkey in 94 years, the AKP of Prime Minister Tayyip Erdoğan, in power since 2002, that has promoted an EU policy most forcefully. In the meantime, a motley alliance of nationalists, both on the right and the left, work to hobble the government on a platform of 'national sovereignty'.

heartlands became a republic under the leadership of Mustafa Kemal Atatürk in 1923.

The Republic and its founder were taboo subjects throughout the 20th century. The 21st has started differently. The legal and emotional barriers no longer seem so tight, and many thinking Turks now feel freer to question the highly nationalistic, anti-liberal underpinnings of their modern state.

Eurasian union?
Turkey has been a candidate for the European Union, née the Common Market, since 1962. A customs union has been in effect since 1996. Battered by Turkish persistence, the EU agreed to start formal membership negotiations in 2005. A flurry of new legislation now brings the country in harness with Europe.

God
Islam is at least nominally the religion of over 99.3 percent of Turkey's population. The Turkish attitude toward religion is more earnest than the British, but somewhat more relaxed than the American. All boys are circumcised. Eating pork is considered unthinkable. But wine – another religious taboo – is freely available everywhere, and praying five times a day as the Quran prescribes is

Photos Nişanyan Gezi Tanitim Ltd

considered behaviour for an eccentric grandmother - or an ambitious politician.

Most women in rural areas keep the head covered: it is considered a requisite of decent dress. In the city, a headscarf can indicate someone who is provincial, traditional or a born-again Muslim. The styling often tells you which.

Build-o-mania

There are times when you imagine every Turk is busy building. The pace of construction is furious along the seaboard and around the cities. New settlements materialize in a matter of months. What you recall as an idyllic hamlet may be a teeming town a decade on. That deserted cove you loved last year may be lost in the landscaping of a 6,000-bed hotel complex next. The buzz and clang of building machinery is everywhere. The small hotels are affected, too: like little boys, they tend to grow fast and a little awkwardly. The eight-year history of this guidebook is littered with formerly charming small hotels that fell victim to their success, yielding to the reckless urge to expand.

All this is partly the result of a magnificently dynamic economy that does not yet have the means to channel savings into large-scale investment. ("We got 20,000 in the safe, dear, let's start a house.") Internal migration, drawing vast numbers from the interior to the coast, and from rural areas to the cities, fuels demand for housing. The rapid change in lifestyles feeds a nation-wide urge to destroy the old to make room for the new. Environmental concerns are dismissed; so are history and tradition. Entire historic towns are wiped away to make way for new growths of cement and breeze-block. Unique natural habitats are destroyed to supply electricity and water and roads to burgeoning cities.

Is it still worth going to Turkey? The answer is an emphatic yes, because there is still so much that remains untouched. And it makes all the more sense to go now – rather than later, when it may be just too late.

History and culture

Photo Turkish Culture and Tourism Office

Getting wheels

Driving around Istanbul is not for the nervous. But apart from the Big City, driving in Turkey is thoroughly enjoyable, and not much less safe than in any other country. This is the considered opinion of your authors, who regularly tread 40,000 kilometres of Turkish tarmac a year. The country is immensely scenic. The roads are mostly in excellent condition. Traffic is sparse except on some main trunk roads, particularly between Istanbul and Izmir. Driving is on the right. Road signs are reasonably good. Traffic police are nice to foreigners. Drivers tend to be a lot more relaxed than in most (west-) European countries. So what if they sometimes overtake that lorry without giving signal?

Renting a car is obviously the most convenient way to go about. All the big international chains are there. Some medium-sized companies like Decar/Thrifty offer the convenience of free drop-off across the country. www.argonautturkey.com/rentacar is a good place to start.

To lock or not to lock

It will take an outsider a few hours or a few days to realise that Turkey is one of the safest countries under the sun in terms of day-to-day risks to personal security and property. A moderate amount of sleaze is to be expected in touristy areas like Istanbul's Sultanahmet Square or Antalya's beaches. Single women may encounter excessive curiosity, often bordering on the intrusive, but it is seldom any worse. As a rule, it becomes safer and friendlier the farther you go from the obvious tourist areas. There are no parts of the country that are 'unsafe' for a foreigner, including the farthest recesses of the east and the poorest neighbourhoods of Istanbul.

Nuisances

A £10 entry charge is levied on all UK nationals entering Turkey. English electrical appliances with a standard three-pin plug will not work in Turkey unless you have an adaptor plug, which, however, is entirely unavailable in the country. English mobile phones, by contrast, work without fuss. The mobile phone network is pervasive: you will catch a signal nearly everywhere except on remote mountainsides.

Charge-free telephones for fire, ambulance, police, etc exist, though no-one in our experience ever uses them. Contact your hotel desk in an emergency. Flag down the first passer-by if your car breaks down in the midst of nowhere. As a rule, you will find civilians nicer and more efficient than officials.

Don't do that

Hooliganism and rude behaviour is less tolerated than in most European countries. Restraint and decorum are expected from a 'guest', though usually people are perfectly willing to smile upon and forgive the foibles of a foreigner.

Discussing politics is a national pastime among Turks, but a foreigner enters the fray at his own risk. As a rule avoid debating Atatürk (you will not hear a sincere word), the Armenians (the gap is too wide), or the Kurds (the PKK war has generated too much bitterness).

Photo Nişanyan Gezi Tanitim Ltd

The unspeakable nation

Twelve to 20 million Kurds are said to live in Turkey. Kurdish — an Iranian language unrelated to Turkish — is the dominant language of the south-eastern corner of the country bordered by the river Euphrates (Fırat) and the mountains south of Erzurum. A third of the Kurdish population lives dispersed across the rest of the country, forming a poor underclass in most towns. There is little overt discrimination against Kurdish individuals so long as they remain mute about their ethnic identity. Being overtly Kurdish is not considered polite.

History and culture

A guerrilla movement led by Kurdish Workers' Party (PKK) ravaged the south-east from the late 80s onward. It was put down around 1999 by the Turkish Armed Forces at the cost of over 30,000 lives.

No more millionaires

The Turkish lira was shorn of its millions in 2005. One dollar is now worth about one and a half new Turkish lira (YTL) rather than a million and a half. You will find a lot of people who still quote prices in the old way, so don't be surprised if a taxi ride costs 20 million, or someone's monthly salary runs into the billions. The old notes remain in circulation until the end of 2006.

Nearly everyone in the country will accept euros and dollars as a matter of course, though sterling is somewhat less familiar. Daily rates are published in all newspapers. Credit cards are readily used even in the hoariest old provincial bazaar. You can use them to draw cash from the ATMs of most banks. There are no relevant limits on the amount of money you can bring into or take out of the country.

Bargaining is practised in the bazaar, though it is nowhere as flagrant as in the other bazaar lands. The general rule is: try what you can where there is no written price, but a price tag usually means what it says.

Photos Turkish Culture and Tourism Office

Language

Pronunciation

Turkey adopted the Latin alphabet in 1928, after 900 years of using the Arabic script. Spelling is highly phonetic, ie. every letter represents one sound, and one sound only, in almost all contexts. There are no diphthongs, and no confusing double consonants.

Vowel values are as in German or Italian, except the undotted ı which sounds like the second vowel in vowel. Stress is usually on the final syllable.

Of the consonants, **c** is always pronounced as in George, **ç** as in church, **g** as in Greg, **ş** as in shish-kebab. **H** is always a distinct sound; **ğ** with a hat simply lengthens the previous vowel — thus tophane is like top-honey and doğan sounds like an exaggerated dawn. Try these words: Kuşadası (coosh-a-dusser), çakır (chuck-er), çiçeği (chichi-yi).

Tongue no bar

Ninety-seven percent of the hotels in this book claim that either the owner or the responsible desk person speaks English, whether perfectly or not. There is no need to apologise at length when you have to address them in the Bard's tongue - if they don't understand you, they'll fetch somebody who does.

Glossary of Turkish words

Merhaba means hallo, and teşekkür ederim (te-shack-cure a-dairy-m) is the tongue-twisting expression of thanks. Everybody knows 'hallo' and 'thank you'.

Baklava A sinfully sweet pastry that comes in a dozen varieties, some bearing graphic names like 'lady's navel' or 'nightingale's nest'. The filling can be walnut or pistachio; hazelnut is considered cheap. The Turks got it from the Syrians, while the Greeks elbowed in much later.

Beton Cement: not only a building material but the mark of a way of life: modern, greedy, pragmatic and contemptuous of beauty. Turkey is the world's fourth largest producer of cement.

Ezan A loud bawl broadcast from the top of minarets that calls the believers to prayer five times a day. The text is in Arabic. Six out of ten Turks do not know what the words mean.

Fasıl A name for classical Ottoman upper-class music, now largely a dead art.

Language

Hamam A Turkish bath, usually lined in marble and heated below the ground. You lounge about freely and splash yourself with pailfuls of hot water. If it is a public bath, there will usually be an attendant who will scrub and knead and soap you for a tip.

İnşallah 'God willing' is the expression that a humble servant of God is supposed to utter every time he makes a statement in the future tense. Example: God willing this bus will go to Antalya, inşallah your steak shall not be burned.

Jandarma The rural police manned by army conscripts. The younger generation of gendarmerie is polite, helpful, intelligent and good-natured to a surprising degree.

Kervansaray Caravanserai in English; a fortified hostel that the sultans of old built to foster the caravan trade. The best date from the 13th century, and line the lonely highways of central and eastern Anatolia at 20-mile intervals.

Kilim A flat-weave carpet, usually in rich tones of red and ochre. The best come from the Kurdish East. They are cheaper than regular tufted rugs, so they used to form the principal ornament of a peasant's house before the arrival of even cheaper machine carpets.

Konak An old-style Turkish house. A proper konak will have kitchens, storerooms and stables on the ground floor. The upper floor will be divided into reception rooms (selamlık) and private rooms reserved for the women and children of the household (harem).

Lokanta A restaurant, usually modest. A restoran is the same thing with pretensions of class.

Meze Cold appetisers served before a meal, typically cooked in olive oil. You will find the same tired old stuff in nine out of ten restaurants, but you will know the difference instantly when you hit the tenth.

Muhtar The village headman, who is elected for a five-year term. It was polite in the past to pay respects to the muhtar on arriving at a faraway village, but this is no longer expected.

Pansiyon Not a retirement benefit but a guest house, or a B&B. The rage for private house-pansiyons, so common in the 70s, all but died out in the sophisticated 90s. When a hotel is named konak, konukevi or han, then you know it is owned by a trendy person from the big city.

Paşa Spelled 'pasha' in English, is a top-ranked official of the Ottoman Empire, the equivalent of a general or government minister.

Rakı The aniseed-flavoured national spirit. It turns white when diluted with water, earning the epithet 'lion's milk'. Properly speaking, rakı accompanies an endless round of cold and warm appetisers, at the end of which you will have little room left for a main course.

Site Pronounced as the French 'cité', site means among other things a housing estate – usually hundreds of identical cubicles deployed in military order like a camp of the invading Martians. The habit spread in the 80s; now every other hill and cornfield along the coast, from Istanbul to Syria, is disfigured by these unsightly growths.

Sütlaç A sweet rice pudding made with milk and usually burned slightly to obtain a caramelised top. The best sütlaç is made around the town of Maçka in the Black Sea mountains.

Yalı A simple waterfront, though what first comes to mind is one of those gorgeous waterfront residences that Ottoman big shots once built along the Bosphorus.

Yayla A highland settlement with lots of pasturage. People used to migrate with their flocks to the yayla in summer. The habit of moving to high places in summer persists in parts of the country, notably the Black Sea region and the Taurus Mountains.

BALLOONING IN CAPPADOCIA

Few places on earth are more suited to ballooning than Cappadocia. The crazy topography is a floater's delight. The area is compact enough to pack an amazing number of wows into a two-hour flight. And the weather is uniformly perfect throughout the summer.

The couple that made hot-air ballooning almost synonymous with Cappadocia are Kaili, an Englishwoman, and her Swedish partner Lars. They offer an impressively choreographed show, which earns top marks for the details – all the way from hotel pick-up service to the farewell champagne. And if you feel like some fruit, why, they will float just low enough to pick you some apricots from the branch.

It would be a pity to come this far and miss the experience.

Cappadocia Balloons
Kaili Kidner & Lars-Eric Möre
Göreme, Cappadocia
www.kapadokyaballoons.com
fly@kapadokyaballoons.com

Photo Nişanyan Gezi Tanitim Ltd

Fragile Earth series

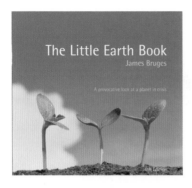

The Little Earth Book
Edition 4, £6.99
By James Bruges

A little book that has proved both hugely popular – and provocative. This new edition has chapters on Islam, Climate Change and The Tyranny of Corporations.

The Little Food Book
Edition 1, £6.99
By Craig Sams, Chairman of the Soil Association

An explosive account of the food we eat today. Never have we been at such risk - from our food. This book will help understand what's at stake.

The Little Money Book
Edition 1, £6.99
By David Boyle, an associate of the New Economics Foundation

This pithy, wry little guide will tell you where money comes from, what it means, what it's doing to the planet and what we might be able to do about it.

www.fragile-earth.com

Six Days

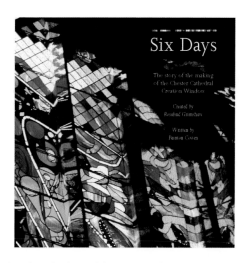

Celebrating the triumph of creativity over adversity.

An inspiring and heart-rending story of the making of the stained glass 'Creation' window at Chester Cathedral by a woman battling with debilitating Parkinson's disease.

"Within a few seconds, the tears were running down my cheeks. The window was one of the most beautiful things I had ever seen. It is a tour-de force, playing with light like no other window ..."
Anthropologist Hugh Brody

In 1983, Ros Grimshaw, a distinguished designer, artist and creator of stained glass windows, was diagnosed with Parkinson's disease. Refusing to allow her illness to prevent her from working, Ros became even more adept at her craft, and in 2000 won the commission to design and make the 'Creation' Stained Glass Window for Chester Cathedral.

Six Days traces the evolution of the window from the first sketches to its final, glorious completion as a rare and wonderful tribute to Life itself: for each of the six 'days' of Creation recounted in Genesis, there is a scene below that is relevant to the world of today and tomorrow.

Heart-rending extracts from Ros's diary capture the personal struggle involved. Superb photography captures the luminescence of the stunning stained glass, while the story weaves together essays, poems, and moving contributions from Ros's partner, Patrick Costeloe.

Available from Alastair Sawday Publishing £12.99

Order Form

All these books are available in major bookshops or you may order them direct.
Post and packaging are FREE within the UK.

British Hotels, Inns & Other Places	£13.99
Bed & Breakfast for Garden Lovers	£14.99
Pubs & Inns of England & Wales	£13.99
London	£9.99
British Bed & Breakfast	£14.99
French Bed & Breakfast	£15.99
French Hotels, Châteaux & Inns	£13.99
French Holiday Homes	£11.99
Paris Hotels	£9.99
Ireland	£12.99
Spain	£14.99
Portugal	£10.99
Italy	£12.99
Mountains of Europe	£9.99
India	£10.99
Morocco	£10.99
The Little Earth Book	£6.99
The Little Food Book	£6.99
The Little Money Book	£6.99
Six Days	£12.99

Please make cheques payable to Alastair Sawday Publishing. Total £ _____

Please send cheques to: Alastair Sawday Publishing, The Home Farm Stables,
Barrow Gurney, Bristol BS48 3RW. For credit card orders call +44 (0)1275 464891
or order directly from our web site www.specialplacestostay.com

Title   First name   Surname
_____
Address
_____

_____
Postcode   Tel

TUR1

If you do not wish to receive mail from other like-minded companies, please tick here n
If you would prefer not to receive information about special offers on our books, please tick here n

Bilingual booking form
Rezervasyon formu

Hotel name:

Date:

Sayın Bay/Bayan:

Otelinizi **Alastair Sawday's Special Places – Turkey** kitabından buldum. Aşağıdaki rezervasyonu yapmak istiyorum:

Name/İsim:

Date of arrival/Geliş tarihi:

Date of departure/Gidiş tarihi:

Total persons/Toplam kişi: Including children/Çocuk:

Rooms as follows/Oda dağılımı:

Double   Twin   Triple   Single

Suite   Apartment

We need transfer from the airport/Havaalanı transferi istiyoruz

Notes/notlar:

Konfirmasyonunuzu aşağıdaki numaraya fakslayabilir veya email gönderebilirsiniz.

Could you send us confirmation of our reservation by faxing this form to the number below or using email.

Confirmed/Konfirme:

Fax No: Email:

Tel No:

Rezervasyon formu - Special Places to Stay – Turkey

Coming soon...

A stunning selection of places to stay in mainland Greece and the islands.

Editor:
Michael Cullen

Publication:
February 2006

Price: £11.99

Pages: 232

Maps:
10 colour maps

ALASTAIR SAWDAY'S
SPECIAL PLACES TO STAY

GREECE

All the sparkle and magic of Greece is here, from the tiniest Cycladic isle to the highest Macedonian mountain.

EDITED BY MICHAEL CULLEN

And high time, too! Our new guide to Greece tempts readers with 200 remarkable places to stay on dozens of islands and on the mainland — including the Peloponnese and the mountains of Epirus. Whether you're planning to be madly busy — or not — here's a choice of memorable places to lay your head, from the budget to the budget-blowing, from whitewashed windmills to cosy mountain refuges. And you'll meet some exceptional people.

Quick reference indices

On Beach
The hotel has direct access to a beach (sea or lake).

North Aegean 35 • 37 • 44 • 49 •
Middle Aegean 51 • 67 •
South Aegean 75 • 76 • 81 • 82 •
84 • 86 • 88 • 89 • 91 • 92 • 93 •
94 • 95 • 96 • 97 • 98 • 109 • 111
• 112 •
Mediterranean 117 • 119 • 120 •
122 • 124 • 130 • 131 • 134 •
East & Southeast 192 •

Near Beach
There is a beach within 5km.

Around Istanbul 23 • 24 • 28 •
North Aegean 31 • 32 • 33 • 34 •
38 • 39 • 40 • 41 • 42 • 43 • 45 •
46 • 47 • 48 • 50 •
Middle Aegean 52 • 53 • 54 • 55 •
56 • 59 • 61 • 62 • 65 • 66 • 68 •
South Aegean 70 • 71 • 72 • 73 •
74 • 77 • 78 • 79 • 80 • 83 • 85 •
87 • 90 • 99 • 100 • 101 • 103 •
104 • 105 • 107 • 108 • 110 • 115
Mediterranean 116 • 121 • 123 •
125 • 126 • 127 • 128 • 129 • 132
• 133 • 135 • 136 • 137 • 138 •
139 • 140 • 144 • 145 • 146 •

Nice Garden
There is an outside space for lounging, in not necessarily manicured gardens.

Istanbul 1 • 8 • 9 • 10 • 14 • 18 •
Around Istanbul 21 • 22 • 24 • 23 •
25 • 27 • 28 • 29 • 30 •
North Aegean 31 • 33 • 35 • 37 •
38 • 39 • 40 • 41 • 42 • 44 • 45 •
46 • 47 • 48 • 50 • 49 •
Middle Aegean 51 • 52 • 53 • 54 •
55 • 57 • 58 • 59 • 61 • 62 • 63 •
64 • 65 • 66 • 68 • 67 •
South Aegean 77 • 78 • 76 • 82 •
74 • 75 • 70 • 71 • 72 • 95 • 96 •
94 • 88 • 89 • 90 • 93 • 91 • 92 •
83 • 85 • 86 • 84 • 87 • 102 • 97 •
98 • 99 • 100 • 103 • 101 • 104 •
106 • 107 • 108 • 111 • 110 • 109 •
112 • 115 • 113 • 114 •
Mediterranean 117 • 116 • 118 •
119 • 120 • 121 • 122 • 123 • 124
• 125 • 126 • 127 • 128 • 129 •
130 • 131 • 132 • 133 • 134 • 135
• 142 • 141 • 136 • 137 • 138 •
139 • 140 • 143 • 144 • 145 • 146
Northwest of Ankara 167 • 166 •
168 • 169 • 171 • 172 •
Cappadocia 160 • 161 • 162 • 159
• 158 • 157 • 156 • 155 • 154 •
149 • 148 • 151 • 153 • 150 • 147
Black Sea 174 • 175 • 176 • 177 •
178 • 179 • 180 • 181 • 182 •
184 • 185 •
North Aegean 43 •
South Aegean 73 •

Wheelchair access
Suitable for wheelchair users.

Istanbul 11 •
North Aegean 34 •
South Aegean 89 • 102 • 107 •
Northwest of Ankara 167 •
East & Southeast 186

Index by place

Index by property name

Index by property name

1 Middle Aegean : Bafa **2**

Agora Pansiyon
Kapıkırı, 48200 Milas, Muğla

3 An enchanting place on the roadless north shore of Lake Bafa, wher the old village of Kapıkırı blends with the ruins of Heracleia-by-Latmos. An extinct volcano rises in the back, hiding the ruins of a dozen mediaeval monasteries in its folds. An islet bearing another Byzantine monastery faces the village beach; it was here that Selene, the moon goddess, fell in love with the shepherd Endymion as he lay asleep by the shore, asked Zeus to grant the youth perpetual sleep and bore 50 children from their nightly encounters. Agora is the last primitive among a handful of rudimentary *pansiyons* that exist in the village. It consists of a few modest bungalows in a flower-filled garden to which several more comfortable 'modern' rooms were added a couple of years ago. Mr Serçin, formerly the village *muhtar*, runs the house with his wife and daughters, still full of eager and erratic hospitality after all these years. There is good fresh seafish from the fisheries of Dalyan, and hiking tours can be organised into the fantastic boulderlands of Beşparmak Mountain upon request.

rooms	14: 11 twins/doubles, 3 cabins, some sharing showers.	**4**
price	Half board 100 YTL. Singles 80 YTL.	**5**
meals	Half board only.	**6**
closed	Never.	**7**
directions	39km from Milas: Söke road, right (northwards) at Çamiçi, 11km to Kapıkırı.	**8**
airport	52km from Bodrum Airport.	**9**

	Orhan Serçin
tel	+90 (252) 5435445
fax	+90 (252) 5435567
email	info@herakleia.com
web	www.herakleia.com

10 Guest house

12

Explanation

❶ region and **❷** visitor destination

❸ write up
Written by the authors after inspection.

❹ rooms
Bedrooms are en suite, unless otherwise stated.

❺ price
The price shown is for two people sharing a room; half board prices are also
for two. A price range incorporates room/seasonal differences.Self-catering
prices are per apartment per night.

❻ meals
Assume breakfast is included in the price, except in self-catering houses. Meal
prices are per person, and generally include wine or beer.

❼ closed
When given in months, this means for the whole of the named months
and the time in between.

❽ directions
Use as a rough guide, check details when booking, and travel with a good
map.

❾ airport
Nearest airport within a 250km radius.

❿ type of property
Hotel, guest house, camp or self-catering.

⓫ map & entry numbers
Catered properties are shown in red on the map pages, self-catering in blue.

⓬ symbols
see the last page of the book for a fuller explanation:

  Ġ   wheelchair facilities

  Ⓚ   easily accessible bedrooms

  ✗   no smoking anywhere

  ▱   credit cards accepted

  guests' pets welcome

  owners' pets live here

  ठ्ठ   bikes on the premises

  👟   information on local walks

  ⚦   air-conditioning in some
            bedrooms

  English spoken

  Pool

  👶   Children welcome

www.specialplacestostay.com

- Britain
- France
- India
- Ireland
- Italy
- Morocco
- Portugal
- Spain...

all in one place!

On the unfathomable sea of online accommodation pages, those who have discovered www.specialplacestostay.com have found it to be an island of reliability. Not only will you find a database full of trustworthy, up-to-date information about all of the places in the series, but also:

- Links to their web sites
- Colourful, clickable, interactive maps
- The opportunity to make most bookings by e-mail
- Online purchasing of our books, securely and cheaply
- Regular, exclusive special offers
- The latest news about future editions and future titles
- Special offers and news from our owners
- News and updates about our books, sent to you by e-mail

Keep an eye out for news and special features that won't appear anywhere else but in our window on the worldwide web.

www.special-escapes.co.uk

Discover your perfect self-catering escape in Britain...

We have launched a brand new self-catering web site. With the same punch and attitude as all our printed guides, www.special-escapes.co.uk celebrates only those places that we have visted and genuinely like – castles, cottages, bothies and more...

Russell Wilkinson, Web Site Manager
website@specialplacestostay.com